World English Literature

A Cosmic Stream of Metalanguage

World English Literature

A Cosmic Stream of Metalanguage

Gauri Shankar Jha

AUTHORSPRESS

Worldwide Circulation through Authorspress Global Network

First Published 2013

by

Authorspress

Editorial

Q-2A Hauz Khas Enclave
New Delhi-110 016

Marketing

E-35/103, Jawahar Park
Laxmi Nagar, Delhi-110 092

e-mails: authorspress@rediffmail.com; authorspress@hotmail.com
Website: www.authorspressbooks.com

World English Literature: A Cosmic Stream of Metalanguage

ISBN 978-81-7273-710-8

Printed in India at Krishna Offset, Shahdara.

Dedication

To my only son who is no more...

Preface

To be candid enough, every one of us has a language of our own, and so is the case with literature. In the case of English literature, we should be conscious of the fact that it belongs to all, for whatever the reason may be—be it the compulsions of colonizers which, finally, evolved into an intrinsic pattern of literature, or a prolonged European stay/ sojourn for education or employment or business, or any other responsible factor. In all cases, English literature, it appears, has acquired a massive proportion, an all-pervasive stature—pulsating in almost all countries of the world. English language has acquired the status of metalanguage and so its wide influence cannot be denied.

Naturally, one has to start with the British literature, and then follows the parade to other parts of the globe. It happened with me, too. I started my first acquaintance with the British literature and then rushed to American literature, Indian Writing in English, Australian literature, etc. The collection of research papers, in this book, delineates my journey to all these literatures/ writings; though they have achieved substantive names these days, they owe a lot to the British literature. The essays in this book entail my curiosity in the various genres of literature of different countries; they also reflect the culture, civilization, emotional constitution and reflective gestures of variety.

It is interesting when we find a British poet, like W. B. Yeats, influenced by an Indian religious text/scripture like *The Bhagavad Gita;* likewise, we have the Indian diasporic poets like Vikram Seth, A. K. Ramanujan and Meena Alexander who voice their agony of exile; Wordsworth essentially suffers in solitude; Keats adheres to the positivity of life; Australian poets throbs with their heart-touching poetry; Jayant Mahapatra and Bibhu Padhi emerge out of regional confinement; and Nissim Ezekiel overrules all poetic sensibility. In the field of plays Dattani and Karnad dominate the scenario of Indian English Drama. And in the field of fiction the American Twenties dominates like anything, E. M. Forster establishes a particular tenet, and V. S. Naipaul sets his own pattern.

Thus, the book has covered all significant junctures of global English writings and signifies its all-pervasive nature, irrespective of culture, civilization and space. In this respect, this book is most readable and comprehensive, and will prove indispensable for the contemporary and future generation of curious individuals in the pursuit of English literature in the worldwide perspective.

Gauri Shankar Jha

Acknowledgements

To an ordinary individual and nonentity like me, publication of a book is, undoubtedly, an enormous and Herculean task. It is the blessings of the Almighty only which keeps me on such assignments and bestows success.

Above all, when I find a generous publisher like Shri Sudarshan Kcherry what else can I aspire but thank him for his kind gesture.

Gauri Shankar Jha

Contents

Plays

Fiction

Poetry

1

Sambavami Yuge Yuge : Yeat's Ardent Call

A re-reading of *The Second Coming* may prove disturbing to anyone of us. Yeats's lamentation over the breakdown of human values, taken as a whole, is not strange, if we take into account temper of the contemporary world and the different voices, that of T.S. Eliot, Ezra Pound, James Joyce, etc., but his final resort to the abstractions of the religion, forces us back to accept traditional tenets as well as to be mindful of our integrity. This, on the other hand, asks us to surrender completely to the 'Will of Heaven'. The present paper seeks to examine Yeats's conclusive optimism for the reconstruction of a human globe devoid of all possible negative constraints.

More than sixty-five years after the death of Yeats we find our globe still groping in the same darkness as it was in the first quarter of the twentieth century. It is marked by disrespect for tradition and an eager wish to try out any new suggestion regarding the nature of man, his personal beliefs, convictions or way to salvation. It is an index of material success and spiritual failure, incurable coward and political venality, highly individualistic and culturally immature, moral failure and utopian zeal, defeat of taboos and restoration of sound sense, contradictions in social values and hypocrisies of democracy, puritan pioneers and utilitarian ethics, neurotic arts and sensual religions, etc. Paradoxically enough it is polemical in all ways.

Yeats does not adhere to the on goings of his contemporary world; he is 'the last of the great Romantics', yet he is complex and passionate. And his humanity, solidity, coherence and constant awareness of the demands of decorum and style is more like the moderns, both religious and scientific. The polimicality of Yeats is to be found in the fact that he is neither orthodoxically religious (like Eliot) nor orthodoxically scientific (like his contemporaries), neither radical Marxist nor Freudian. He has a magical attitude and with his own science and religion he discovers primitive science and primitive religion, evident in *A Vision* propounding his own philosophy that is all inclusive and systematic, fitting together into a broadly meaningful and aesthetically satisfying pattern. *The Second Coming* is such a poem that, denounces and establishes a defined pattern, questioning like Harold Monro,

> What have I done that I should be alive?
> O, can I not forget that I am living?
> How shall I reconcile the two conditions:
> Living, and yet—to die? ('Living', W.W., p.178)

The Second Coming opens with a typical raising theory, running and turning in the widening 'gyre', a typical cyclic process of history continues; civilization keeps on growing and perhaps, it has reached its pinnacle of development where 'falcon' (a common man) does not hear its 'falconer' (creator, God) and everything is shattered, only chaos prevails. It is the stage of complete anarchy, indiscipline and disintegration, perhaps, the end of the system. (प्रलय)

The conflict goes on, within and without, and the 'innocence' is being butchered; the elite society 'lack all conviction' while the worst are 'full of passionate intensity'; this is a rhetorical attack. This is a terrifying picture of the world's situation as Yeats saw it in 1919; the second section of the poem is a shift from pessimism to optimism, a hope for 'revelations'—the second coming, the birth of a rough beast, 'a shape with lion body and a head of a man' (नरसिंह) as a saviour of mankind, to bring about a new civilization, for redemption of the entire humanity, similar to Blake's 'Tyger' that astonishes everyone, but is mighty enough to do anything. And there is a possibility of a complete transformation, the end of a civilization and the birth of a new one, with hope and potential, and perhaps, with a commitment too!

It happens so—in every religion—call it, 'incarnation', 'avtar', 'resurrection', 'revelation', or anything else. In Hinduism it has been reiterated: in the *Bhagavad Gita*, it is, यदा यदा हि धर्मस्य ग्लानिर्भवति भारत। अभ्युत्थानमधर्मस्य तदात्मानं सृजाम्यहम्।। In the *Ramcharitmanas*, it is '*Jab jab twin dharm ki hani/Barhe, dusta, adharm.*

Yeats quotes it from Christianity; he believes that Christianity has not achieved what it should have in two thousand years and so the doom's day is near; it is imminent, and 'slouches towards Bethlehem to be born'. Graham Martin is of the view that,

> Yeats seems to have combined a very powerful sense of immediate history with a restricted historical equipment for relating present insight to the determining part Yeats has tried to generalize his immediate foreboding into a historical statement, but since the historical ideas ('gyre') is itself over simple, it simply ratifies the confusions of fear and hope from which the poet begins. (243)

However, Yeats is different as he questions his own prophecy; the last sentence of *The Second Coming* is interrogation, it is not assertive and the reader is in dilemma to infer the exact intention of the poet behind such projections. The 'uncertain tone' and the 'unjustified variation of intensity in the rhetoric' reflect the element of doubt in the poet's mind; this again refers back to his Irish background, the bickering and the unevenness, both hope and tear, an ambiguous approach. That of, loyalties and predispositions. Precisely. Yeats's concept of second coming is simply prediction of a probable future, that is, more elaborate in *A Vision.*

This process of 'eternal recurrence', of demolition of an exhausted civilization and birth of a new one, is an old formula that keeps the world going; it offers a kind of earthly immortality, an amazing illustration of the contracts between the European and Oriental temperaments, a sort of great wheel of existence. Salvation, or *Moksha* or self's ultimate escape of Hinduism and Buddhism is based on such concept that ultimately deny the mundane and call for '*Brahma Satyam, Jagat Mithya*', '*Buddham Sharanam Gachchami*'. Yeats has been influenced by Vico, Nietzsche and Spengler in formulating this theory. It has been established that after reaching certain stage of development human society/civilization is bound to collapse into primitivism; analogous is the case of Marxism which does not guarantee the revetal of a classless society to a society of class as primitive classless society have done in the past. In simple words, it is a sheer curiosity about the past that has developed into an elaborate and all inclusive philosophy of history, at the same time it is self-contradictory too, as the growing spirit of rationality is responsible for both material and moral progress. H.G. Wells has the same curiosity about the future at the end of the 19th century and Walter Scott in the beginning of the 19th century; G.B. Shaw postulates his theory of 'Life Force' (a sort of immanent deity'), that is like a divine spirit, working and moving in human history, for the eternal progression of human race.

Yeats is guided by the esoteric philosophy of history whereas the school of Eliot has definite and orthodox religious belief, and so can never imagine of man as God to function as an agent of change, a transformation or redemption. His vision and philosophic speculations come out of the subjugation of art to personal experiences. He feels that man is entirely responsible for the absurdities of the real world because his attempts to rationalize life thorough scientific investigation and Christian morality have failed. His indignant rejection of philosophy and science is revealed in his mockery of Plotinus and Plato in *The Tower*. In *Nineteen Hundred and Nineteen* he elaborates his concept of the twentieth century nowadays as dragon-ridden, the nightmare! Rides upon sleep. He rejects Christianity in *Vacillation*: "Homer is my example and his unchristened heart / the lion and honey comb, what has scripture said?" Homer is the unchristianed individual as a symbol of attainable unity between man and a veritable spiritual essence.

Both Vico and Nietzsche have influenced Yeats in forming the idea that history is a fated and eternally recurrent pattern and we have to play our assigned roles. Yeats nourishes the contradictory notions of a passionate lust for life and an earnest desire for contemplative immortality of pure, withdrawn spirit. It is the direct consequence of despair and anguish of the contemporary world, out of collapse of settled, traditional and religious order; he digs deep into primitive necessity of the birth of a new civilization. Such call is available in almost all religions of the world. It may be taken as a nostalgiac attempt to solve the prevalent complicacy.

Such call is an escape where an artist visualizes the reconstruction of human civilization, be it Moore's 'Utopia', Yeats' 'Byzantium', Eliot's 'Magi', or the agent, such as Yeats'

'Rough Beast', Shelley's 'West Wind', Shaw's 'Life Force and Superman', Blakes's 'Tyger', Vyas's 'Krishna' and Tulsi's 'Ram'. We have history of avatars and a good array of reformatory idols—a completely optimistic point of view.

References

Green, D., (ed.), 1985, *Winged Words*, Macmillan, New Delhi.

Martin, G., (1984), "The Later Poetry of W.B. Yeats", *The New Pelican Guide to Literature*, Dais Ford (ed.), Penguin Books.

2

Vikram Seth: A Liberal Humanist

With his *Two Lives* as the hot cake of the day, Vikram Seth, once again, is in the news. We fail to decide what we should call him, a poet-novelist or a novelist-poet, for he is successful in both the genres. He step into the poetic world with *Mappings* (1980), and then came *All You Who Sleep Tonight* (1990), *Beastly Tales from—Here and There* (1991), *The Humble Administrator's Garden* (1985), *Three Chinese Poets* (1992), etc. His name came into prominence with his second volume of poetry, *The Humble Administrator's Garden,* that was awarded the Commonwealth Poetry Prize for Asia. Seth, though, designated variously, bases his poetic talent on the exploration of the element of humanism and this paper focuses on the same.

His first poetic work *Mappings* establishes him as a transnational poet caught between the two: India and the rest of the world, their culture, values, etc. The dual feelings of nostalgia for his own land and fascination for the rest of the world tortures him. Like all important creative writers his writing is moulded by his wanderous nature, having no particular inclination towards any specific trend. Like all diasporic writers his writings suffer from the common lapses, at the same time his tendency to dwell on all sorts of flowers to make the sweetest honey is evident in his bulk of writing. M. K. Naik calls it "a bright young man's attempt at self-scrutiny, the 'mappings of his diverse selves.' (171)

The Humble Administrator's Garden, the award-winning book, has three distinct sections of his poetic experience of India, China and America, revealing his aesthetic sense, his Wordsworthian thirst for beauty, Keatsian perception of beauty as joy and, above all, his rejection of Coleridgian daydream of idealism; that is why he questions "What do scruples know of beauty anyway ?" (HAG) and establishes his final verdict, "This is the loveliest of all gardens." (HAG) This collection of poetry is a land where strangers meet in the beginning, and in the end, and discloses his diasporic dislocation, though he denies it vehmently. He strolls in the garden of ideology as a true socialist, perhaps in search of larger humanity, and the old man of 'A Little Night Music' like the old mariner of Coleridge's *The Ancient Mariner* gathers maturity in the end "as if all men/were brothers within the enclosing seas". In 'The North Temple Tower' and 'The Gentle Waves Pavilion', the two meet, the young boys and the lovers. In 'The North Temple Tower', we have,

> Sudden delight: they point upwards and scowl
> One imitates a baby elephant
> The other glares and totters like and owl
> Then stomping through flower-beds with glee.

In 'The Gentle Waves Pavilion', the two lovers meet and behave as they should, yet their unintentional acts are fatal to trees:

> Two lovers come
> To gaze at fish and foreigner in the park
> With a pen-knife hack their names through bark,
> For posterity.

As we know, Seth undertook a trip to China when he was a student at the Nanjing University, China (1980-82) and this visit has a substantial impact on his *The Humble Administrator Garden* career of creativity; it could produce *Three Chinese Poems* and a travelogue *From Heaven Lake.* In the present collection of poems under discussion, the title poem has the portrayal of the Chinese art, in all its manifestations. It does not matter whether the creator of the garden is a corrupt administrator or a maligned character, what matters is his humility that could create such a beautiful garden: "He may have got/The means by somewhat dubious means, but now/This is the loveliest of all gardens." (HAG II) Seth is of the view that the purpose of art is to provide pleasure, as Keats says, "Beauty is a thing of joy for ever; in the same way we should enjoy the beauty of the garden caring least about its source of creations, the output is important not its resource; it is like redefining the concept of art. Yet he feels himself 'an amateur' in "From a Traveller", "Though of course my professional opinion is not what you require/so much as an explication of my status/ as amateur" (HAG. 22); to achieve 'a balanced power', he amalgamates 'obvious', 'obtuse' and 'obscene' with a bit of humour and irony; it is a sort of defining his own poetry and craftsmanship. Seth's concern for culture and heritage, history and mankind, education and administration, religion and art is enormous and its status in communist states is available in *The Great Confucian Temple, Suzhou,* where renovation of temple, concern for culture call of heritage, education of students and lifestyle of common is dictates by leaders and so ridiculous, and "proclaims the oppressive heritage is dead." *The Accountant's House* has Seth's soft corner for aggrieved individual and astonishment at crafted smile, and his *Research Jiangsu Province* is simple "fact and facts".

It is remarkable to note that *The Great Confucian Temple, Suzhua,* surveys the bottleneck in the progression of humanity, *The Accountant's House* sympathize with the beraved family and *Research in Jiangsu Province* has marring effect of emotional section of self by the overpowering, influencing, factual world. He laments over the luxury of not needing to compromise.

His liberal worldview can be read in his opening poem "Profiting", the Indian section "Neem" where he dissolves his own self and becomes along a non-entity, being swayed away to tragic nothingness: "In wreathes of ache and strain/the bent rheumatic potter/constructs his forms from pain"; it is how the process of formation of art goes on; art is the name of continuous sacrifice prolonged surrender and unbearable pang. Seth's diasporic self cries a homeless Indian middle class and thereby anxious for belongingness in his poem "Homeless": 'I envy those/who have a house of their own —when night comes, to lie down in peace/ To know that I may die as I have slept'.

In *All You Who Sleep Tonight* (1990) we have some more instance of Seth's liberal attitude and human endeavour, for instance in the poem "In Other Voices", he goes back to history, and like a perfect post-colonial talks of the subalterean, the suppressed voice from the history, those who suffered in Auschwitz, Lithuania, etc., in the World War II and in the violence and horror of the West; in the guise of Doctor he articulates and rushes to the Almighty for rescue, in "Lithvania" "Beasts of the forest and voracious wolves/Who hasten to spill innocent blood and kill/The pious and the upright. Read these words/But think of Moses' words, the man of God/Sign aloud, O you nations of His people/For he avenges the blood of his servants, and/Renders revenge upon His adversaries" (AYWST, 164)

As a sound philanthropist, his disquietude lies with Hiroshima and Nagasaki, Jews and German, and the entire humanity in general in his 'Work and Freedom', 'A Doctor's Journey', 'Entry for August 6, 1945' and 'Ghalib, Two Years After the Mutiny' bear the same scare,

> The children of high lords go begging in the Street,,..
> That some strange thing has stripped us of our cloths.
> How could she know what lay so heavily on me....

This horrible design of the world ushers him to the world of loneliness, "As if aloneness were a sign/Or greater wisdom in design/To bear the torque of rue and mine." (208) However, their solitude does not deter him because he ascertains it as a begetter of self-discovery and self-knowledge 'Above all, to my heart I'm true' (211); and he captures the certitude that he should not groan long for the fact, 'Know that you aren't alone/The whole world shares your tears.' (213) Seth retrieves an explication in Forster's 'connect' and Coleridge's 'love'; his Golden Gate Bridge connects man to God, artist to art and lover to beloved 'Across God's natural world'. Love enables one to survive in this dreaded world; in the poem 'Soon' he says,

> Stay by my steal word bed
> And hold me where I lie
> Love me when I am dead
> And do not let medic. (AYWST, 173)

P. Dhanaval in his paper titled 'The Humanistic Vision of Girish Karnad' compiled in the book titled *Contemporary India Literature in English* defines humanism as, "Certain cherished human ideals and values such as understanding, benevolence, compassion, mercy, fortitude, judgement, prudence, eloquence, love of honour, kindness, liberty, equality, fraternity, democracy, social justice". (77) And Vikram Seth's poems cover all these connotations. As we know, ours is an age of interrogations: interrogations of all human ideas which is an essential aspect of all humanists dealing with the question of man in the universe. And so, is Seth afraid of relationship, afraid of friendship, afraid of life and afraid of death—where to get the panacea? Where to get the shelter? Where to get solace? He wanders from post to pillar as a loner, "They have left me the quiet gift of fearing/I burn/By night, by day. I tremble". Our life has become a trial of tribulations: no love and no hope only fear and despair. To him, the most comfortable relationship, that is, friendship also appears to be under threat, 'melting us into stores'. In The *Golden Gate* his protagonist ask "If I died, who'd be sad?" Despite his long questionnaire, he goes back to the shelter of the four lettered word 'love' as L.L.Narayan opines:

> The book is a lyrical composition with variations on the theme of love, its forms, degrees and dimensions... both love and its definitions are elusive. Is love is the perfect round to these broken arcs... this multidimensional emotion both in historicity and its contemporary. Love is a reaching between man and man....(p.178)

This love is fragile and can be found everywhere in the form of parental love, maternal love, romantic love, friendship, generosity, devotional love, etc.; at the same time it is the only bond that keeps us alive, and will be so in future. The novel presents characters who initiate their life with rigidity, mistrust and selfishness and culminates in greater ambience of courtesy, kindness, concern and caring', a move towards greater love; "A man must have... someone to love" (6:13); the general consensus is "Anyone will do/For love and who may love us too (1:36); an impossible demand for a rationalist "... love's whole/or else in nothing." (8:35)

Precisely, Seth's poetry stands for his liberal humanist approaches though contradictory reactions prevail in the literary world: Khushwant Singh predicts him 'to be in the Nobel laureate's race'; C.D.Narsimhaih dismisses him as "Seth has only confirmed on the astheric plane, the growing menace of Americanization of the Indian intellectual in life and its values." (120) It is the ambivalence of the Indian situation that torments such poets and we have Nissim Ezekiel encapsulating "boring miniatune of suburban and urban existence" (Entertainment), Daruwalla's displeasure, "Sorry, we can't lay on these days/a suttee-display in the flesh for you"(To Writers Abroad') and Mahapatra's "Endless crow noises." (Dawn at Puri) K.C.Baral is of view that Seth's "endeavour of concerned humanism characterizes not only good poetry, but great poetry". S.Prasannranjan in his article "Intimately in History' opines:

> Seth is worthy of that literary space currently occupied by writers like Elie Wiesel, W.G.Sebald and Primo Levi.... If we cannot eschew hatred, at least, let us eschew group hatred. May we see that we could have been born as each other. May we, in short, believe inhuman logic and perhaps, in due course, in love....History may not answer the last prayer of the humanist as the lives lived and killed, in this genre.... still the world regains a little more humanity—and literature a lost more. (*IT* Sept.19, 2005)

Seth is the only artist who brings personal and historical to perfect textual harmony and 'soap operatic variety in life and manners', called as 'some kind to Tolstoy and his work a Taj Mahal in print'.

References

Naik and Narayan, 2001, *Indian English Literature, 1980-2000*, Penecraft.

Narayan, L.L., "The Golden Bridge is Falling", compiled in *Critical Responses, Commonwealth Literature*, Dept. of English, Osmania Univ., Hyderabad, Sterling Pub., Delhi.

Seth, V., 1986, *The Golden Gate*, O.U.P., Delhi.

______ , *The Humble Administrator's Garden*, O.U.P., Delhi.

______ , *All You Who Sleep Tonight*, New Delhi, Penguin.

Narsimhaiah, C.D. 1995., *Essays on Commonwealth Literature*, Delhi, Penecraft.

3

Australian Poetry : "To the Heart of You All"

Even a casual survey of Australian poetry provides an impression that it is natural, simple and basic as one's lifestyle might be, and yet it stands unique in the world literature for Its all-inclusive nature; it is simply, as Sarojini Naidu says of poetry in general, "Oh, what is that comes to a poet is, it comes to the heart of you all". My paper attempts to evince those ingredients that make it an organic whole, for which I have taken the recent poets like John Kinsella, Allan Wearne, Gig Ryan, Chris Wallace Crabbe, Diane Fahey, Judith Bishop, Anthony Lawrence, Evan Jones, Jill Jones, Meeta Chatterjee, James McAuley, A.D Hope, Francis Hackney, J.B. Cripps, Meg Beckett, etc.

Life and death, love and hate, blessing and disaster—these have been the themes of all poetry of all literature. Perhaps, this is the first innate outburst of a common man untouched by any sort of complexities. Like Indian English poetry, the modernity could invade it a bit late, as K. Satchidanandan writes,

> The trauma of modern experience of finding ourselves in an environment that promises us adventure, power, joy, growth, transformation of ourselves and the world, and at the same time threatens to destroy everything we have, everything we know, everything we are and this pours us into a maelstrom of perpetual disintegration and renewal, of struggle and contradiction, of ambiguity and anguish had hit the Indian psyche rather late. (Satchidanandan, XXX, 2000.)

The first instinctive outpouring is that of the surroundings, the nature, its deeds and misdeeds,

> How silent this sunlit world,
> A single leaf
> Falls from the frangipani tree
> I hear it settle on the dewy grass.
> In the hushed stillness
> I seem to sense the growth to face the light atoms re-energized.
> (Hackney. *Replica*, p.7)

The mind and the body work in union, revealing the Dionysian ego for the simple reason that these poets live in consonance with nature, consequently, life is neither so modern (complex) nor so frenzied. Patricia Prime has a nice observation regarding such poets:

> Poets.... write poetry that involves, thinking in solitude, dreaming of images, meditating on meanings, and writing down what comes to mind. Thinking gets fuelled from reading literature, history, the science, philosophy, and reading the works deemed to be essential within the culture. Reading provides the connective issue between the past and future... these poets are among writers I like to read, sharing as they do, their free-hearted art, which is life itself. (*Creative Forum,* Vol.13, No.1, 2 Jan-June 2000, p.6)

Naturally, the first shelter of all these poets is nature itself, and the affinity towards it brings one closer to the creator and spirituality appears and reappears. Frances Hackney may be quoted in this regard:

> Drenched in the moons transforming light
> the garden shimmers to unearthly glory,
> as though the hem of Eternity's Veil were raised.
> (Poet, *Moonlight*, Vol.42, No.8, p.31)

In another poem titled 'Incompatibility' he says:

> When, side by side, we view the midnight sky,
> You see only stars. 1 see the pollen dust
> of God's vast flowering, the sacred sperm
> that fertilizes faith and poetry.
>
> (*Poet*, Vol.42, No.2, p.42)

And the ulterior desire:

> Lord, may the stillness of my sprit
> become the mirror of your Love.
>
> (*Poet*, Vol.43, No.1, p.53)

It happens with everyone of us and so with the poet too: we observe our surrounding; we are happy with the pleasing happenings of nature and we are amazed at the happenings that appear to be out of tune. The sunrise, the moonlight, the blooming of flowers, the butterflies, the chirping birds make us happy whereas the devastating cyclone appears inhuman. Meg Beckett cries,

> I watch the might of nature ride
> spurred in anger
> to the cringing fringe of land
> basso proundo is your partner
> in crime to howl and rage in destruction. King tides flood the
> catchment area as saturated man and beast struggle to survive.
>
> (*Poet*, Vol.43, No.2, p.37)

Through the devastating nature we enter the complexity of human life, human relationship and the social fabrication. Beckett moans at the demand of big cities in his 'Metropolis',

> My thought a frozen volcano of hatred
> sought escape among the innocent eucalypts......
> the city antagonist held me captive
> a sacrificial lamb on the alter of commerce.
>
> (*Poet*,Vol 43, No.1, p.44)

Still there is hope. We came to know the contrary design of nature, the coexistence of the opposites, the relevance of day compared to night, of light compared to darkness, of sunrise compared to sunset, virtue compared to vice, and so on and so forth; and hence we are hopeful, as Frances Hackney is in his 'Dawning',

> It is the Lord himself who comes
> riding the wings of the incandescent sun
> to bring to us the ancient miracle
> of nascent tomorrow and ascendant hope.
>
> (*Poet*, Vol. 42 No.1, p.6)

and in the *Moonlight* F. Hackney glimpses the first love,

> ... inviting me to glimpse, for these few moments
> how Eden must have looked to Eve
> on her first night after creation.
>
> (*Poet*, Vol.42, No.8, p.31)

F. Hackney can see his 'marvel at its diverse complexity' and carves for a better future in his poem 'Tomorrow',

> Lord, tomorrow when I wake
> let me look from my window and see the world
> as for the first time
> and if that day I chance to meet a friend
> Let me look into that other's eyes
> with joy and gratitude,
> seeing in their kindness, God.
>
> (*Poet*, Vol.41, No.12, p.7)

Hackney can visualize the whole world with gratitude as his pretty creation; he grows mysterious and visionary like Blake in his poem 'Incompatibility',

> A new rose opens just outside your door
> pretty you say; just continue on your way

Without a pause. To me her petal led lips
breathe of life's mystery, of Beauty's Power
that cannot be explained....
One day, beside the sea, I thought I saw
a brief awareness of same deeper truth
behind your eyes. But, transient as foam,
it faded as it dawned.

(*Poet,* Vol. 43, No.1, p.53)

The poet is in search of Truth in the layers of creation, but the ultimate is beyond reach and its mysterious stature all immunized. He further asks,

What do you hear
When Mahlur's music fills the concert hall
And I hold back the tears, which you nod off?
Your universe is not my universe.

(*Poet,* Vol.42, No.2, p.42)

The gap between the poet and Lord remains wide; the poet's anxiety to fill it up fails; the agency of separation is revealed in tears, and the merger of humanity with the ultimate appears to be impossible; it is simply the height of spirituality and nothing else. Like Tagore he suffers and like Wordsworth he advances just for unison or amalgamation to reach perfection. J.B. Cripps 'Sun Moon Lake' reminds us of Hindi Chhayavadi poet Sumitranand Pant and his poems 'Nauka Vihar' where Pant relishes the boat journey in a river in moonlit night,

the long boat slid through the waters
rains dimpled the lake surface, mountains
and temples, rose up out of the low cloud
.... place of peace.

(*Poet,* Vo.42, No.1, p.16)

Prof. Cripps's main concern is peace for the entire humanity: "That all humans/Hopefully can achieve the voice of peace". He has coined a unique formula to achieve 'freedom through peace', as Braithwaite talks of 'discipline through freedom' in 'To Sir With Love, the novel that intends to correct both teachers and students. Such images came only in snatches and these poets air their opinions or feelings triggered by circumstances and sensation, true and pure of thought leading to poetry as a stream of words with a purpose. Nature is the first option.

Justice S. Mohan in his speech delivered at World Congress of Poet, Sydney, Australia in October 2001, says,

> There is a poem on every form of tree or flower, but poetry which lives in the trees and flowers of Australia differs from that of other countries some see no beauty in our trees without shade, our flowers without perfume, and birds that cannot fly, and our beast that have not yet learned to walk on our flours. But the dweller in the wilderness acknowledges the subtle charm of the fantastic land of monstrosities. He becomes familiar with the beauty of loneliness. (*Poet*, Vol.42, No.12, p.2)

With the advance in civilization complicacy in human life multiplies and consequently the attention of the poet shifts to such junctures with sheer bewilderment. In 'The Juniper Tree' Diane Fahey tells us,

> There is a place beneath
> the world's tree where the deepest grief
> and wrongs go...
> wrong is set right, the death under,
> and all who suffered receive balm
>
> (*JLA*, Vol. 1, No. 1, p.198)

This world and its people are product of the choice and options that they prefer to adopt and Gig Ryan reminds us, "Beautiful friends/what can I say when you writhe/about choice" (195) and she further makes a proposition: "The works don't hang anyone/

They wallow in their primitive fables/diligent acolytes/who pulls me into the worlds."(196) Dr. John Hawke, in his article titled "Contemporary Australian Poetry: An Introduction" admits that as an outsider reader we look for colonial themes of pastoral and rural life, and the vestiges of convictism which can he called 'imperial' readings of Australian poetry but 'introversion' is the specialty of this poetry which remains the direct consequences of 'self-referentiality'. He further admits that Australia exports its sports stars and scientists but keeps its wine and poetry by itself and this provides the final moorings to its literature.

One feels that Jill Jones has not only paralleled her stature with Wordsworth but somehow surpassed him in her poem 'Drawing Breath',

> Horizon closes
> but the road is long.
> Forgotten
> Skies touch rises
> Purple flowers of night
> Jasmine on fences
> night cool nostalgia.
> Remember hands
> the Full ride drift
> wet waiting arms.
> Drowned green
> Kisses across a river
> And light steps of spring rains
> tracing the hill
> drawing breath.

Jill Jones has assimilated herself with the being of nature and in 'The Valley' something unusual happens, "the rain is burnt/wind is heavy the falling stars of history prayer bows silent only blood is avid". Such is the charm of Australian poetry: it runs deep in our veins.

However, Australian poetry is not completely divorced from the ongoing of the world, the complicacy of the human mind, human relationship and social hazards, and so Judith Bishop observes: "But the flesh of a man/who has lost divine lightness/is so heavy/that the angles/have relinquished the task/and his body falling". And Chris Wallace Crabbe in his poem 'At the Cloth Line' admits, "Every thing slips away too soon/yet something leaves its mark here like? A rainbow ring around the moon"; he questions deliberately, "What is the use of grief? Its only a blind wind sowing the sand with sand/and so is music."

We Indians go for *rasa* (delightness) in literature as per our ancient aestheticians prefer to call it and consequently poets look at man and the world as a whole as manifested in myriads of different varieties of shapes and shades and in various amalgams of feelings, emotions, complexities and contradictions. They peer into the cone of truth and experience it with an innate, an insatiable craving for power and for beauty. French critic Tame believes that literature must be evaluated on the basis of the simple formula of placing the writer in the context of his race, the milieu and moment. On the basis of this assumption, it has been argued that the men of Heroic Age created the Epic; the men of a city contend that the sophisticated age evolved the drama; the industrial age which began in the nineteenth century gave the novel a terrific vogue, and the technological demi-paradise of the twentieth century has been responsible for the detective stay, the swift film script and the bright television show. Though it is a sweeping generalization, it has some elements of truth, and Australian poetry falls in the same category. No doubt, Sophacles, Aristophanes, Kalidasa, Bhavabhuti, Shakespeare and Moliere were men with pronounced individuality of their own, it should be realized that literature is not merely a social or racial product, the eruption of particular geographical region, the precipitate thrown by the Time Sprit; on the other hand, it is the creation of sundry men and women driven by their demons, racked by their pains and fears, sustained by their dreams and visions. In fact, both man and literature have a dual quality, he is both walled within and an isolated speck; he is verily unique; he is one with all the generation of Adam, a part of all that he has met, an atomic constituent of the Cosmos; a piece of literature, even a single phrase, is a marvel, a star in its own right governed by its own law, a flicker that is a part of a continuous phenomenon. Australian poetry stands on its own but very much in consonance with the world literature by divulging its heart to all, and nature is no more a sympathetic shelter, rather a routine practitioner: "At nightfall, the sky and land meet like two wounded saints too scared to sleep." ("Landscape" Meeta Chaterjee, *JLA* p.203)

References

Hackney, Frances, 'A Windless Morning' *Replica*, Vol. VIII, No.1. p.7.
Prime, P., 'Introduction' *Creative Forum*, Vol.13, No.1-2, 2000, p.6
Poet, Vol.42, No.8.
______ Vol. 42, No.2
______ Vol. 43, No.1
______ Vol. 43, No.2
______ Vol. 41, No.12
______ Vol. 42, No.1.
______ Vol. 42, No.12
______ Vol.1, No.1
Satchidanandan, K., (ed.), *Signatures*, N.B.T., New Delhi, 2000.

4

Ramanujan, the Diaspora Priest

While reading Girish Karnad the outstanding playwright of Indian English Writing, the name of A. K. Ramanujan recurs most frequently, not as his companion but as his guide who helped him to comprehend the intellectual panorama of the Indian culture. Karnad is immensely indebted to Ramanujan's "Intellectual insight", he quotes his exchanges with him. A. B. Dharwadkar writes in the Introduction of *Collected Plays* (Vol.II):

> At an intertextual level quite removed from the public life of the play, *Tale-Danda*, is also an extended tribute to A.K. Ramanujan, and the culmination of a long-standing intellectual relationship between the two leading post-independence authors from Karnataka. Karnad was drawn to his older contemporary from early adulthood because Ramanujan's brilliance as a poet, translator and scholar of Tamil and Kannada literature seemed to offer an exemplary mode) as well as an antithesis to his own interest as a playwright... he sometimes jocularly describes his entire creative carrier as an attempt to give antistic form to Ramanujan's intellectual insight.... Dedicated the 1989 English translation of *Naga-Mandala* to Ramanujan in acknowledgement not only of the folktales he had passed along but the rich conversation between them that had circled endlessly around oral culture, folklore... through translation and commentary Ramanujan had accomplished the first major recuperation of this premodern socio-religious and literary movement... in *Tale-Danda* Karnad breathed a different kind of life into poetic texts and historical events by developing a dramatic structure that would 'explain'

> the relation of poetry and religious mysticism.... Following his mentor's example, he also avoided the sentimental simplifications... (XIV-XV)

Such was the influence of Ramanujan over Karnad who is also taken to be a great intellectual of the day.

Ramanujan spent his three decades of life in the United States and yet had persistent obsession with his 'Indian part' (82), that is why I prefer to term him as a diasporic priest. He grew up in a traditional middle-class southern-brahmin family and possessed a bitter memory of 'a basketful of ritual cobras'. Though deeply immersed in the conventional design he does not accept everything blindly and yet as a diasporic entity he craves for his roots. As Shiv K. Kumar points out, "to the modern poet reality comes filtered through a juxtaposition of paradoxes." (3) We may cite the instance of 'Another view of Grace' where we may very easily diagnose the East-West clash or say the clash of two 'distinctly polarized patterns of culture'.

> Bred Brahmin among singers of shivering hymes
> I shudder to the bore at hungers that roam the streets
> beyond the constables beat. But there she stood
> upon that dusty rood on a nightlit april mind
> and gave me a look. Commandments crumbled
> in my fathers past. He tumble hair suddenly known
> as silk in my angry hand, I shook a little
> and took her behind the laws of my land.
>
> ('Another View of Grace')

Ramanujan feels the encounter of the two cultures within him "the Oriental which upholds restraint and the Western which permits unrestrained sexuality in the name of individual freedom." (3) He, as an inhibited brahmin, finds himself helpless and his defence ecrumbling when he faces an American lady in the street, a foreign female with a lot of attraction. It is a sort of irony distinctly available in the post-Independence Indian English poetry, disturbing all facts of human experience—social, religious, moral or political. He is out to connect, that is, he believes in the wholeness of mankind, something like *Vasudhaiva Kutumbakam*, a sort of globalization, unification of the whole mankind; in his poem 'Connect' this voice can be heard,

> Connect! Connect—Cries my disconnecting
> Madness, resembling phrases.
> See the cycles.
> Connect, beast with monks, slave economics and
> the golden bough.

He cannot betray his tradition, the ethics of Hinduism calls him ever; the title poem of the 'Second Sight' puts it clearly.

> You are a Hindoo, aren't you?
> You must have a
> Second Sight.

He is a man who prefers to remain down-to-earth with his family, society, history, mythology, nature and associates; his wide and extensive study reading does not believe in isolation but companions. Family is his point of attraction: he recalls his grandfather in the poem titled 'Extended Family' and swears not to be "dependent/on several people/yet to come". Interestingly, he perceives three generation of women, that is, mother/wife and daughter in linear-progression, in his poem titled 'Love Poem for a Wife and Her Trees.' In 'Looking for the Centre', his endeavour is to trace the genesis, call it root or seed, but he finds it a difficult task,

> Suddenly, connections severed
> as in a lobotomy, unburdened
> of history, I lose

> my bearings, a circum Zilla Spun
> at the end of her rope, dizzy
> terrified
> and happy...

In the poem 'Watefalls in a Bank', he trades back to his country,

> As I transact with the past as with another
> country with it own customs, currency,
> stock exchange, always
> at a loss when I count my change.

He is fond of myths and mythology which have fabricated the rich texture of Hindu religious, acripture, culture and civilization. Thus, in 'Mythologies 1', we find the theory of salvation or *moksha* of a demon when killed by God, and here is Purana myth,

> The child took her breast
> in his mouth and sucked it right out of her chest
> Her carcass stretched from North to South
> She changed, undone by grace
> from deadly mother to happy demon
> found life in death.

In the same way, in the poem 'Mythologies 2' Ramanujan shows the salvation of a man who is killed by Lord Visnu though he had the boon of not to be killed by demon, God, or beast, not by day or night, by no manufactured weapon, not out of doors or inside, not in the sky nor on earth; this killing is symbolic of the end of the evil whatever its form may be, and the triumph of the just,

> Come now, come soon,
> Vishnu, man, lion, ṇeither and both, to hold
> him in your tap to disembowd his pride
> with the steal glint of bare claws at twilight.

Ramanujan has an astounding command over the vast treasure of Indian myths and folklore which formed the theme of bulk of his poetry a significant trait of post-colonial literature. It is this wide knowledge that bestows unambiguity to his world of creativity and could allure a titan like Girish Karnad, who quotes him to make the past relevant,

> Even in a large modern city like Madras, Bombay or Calcutta, even in Western-style nuclear families with their well-planned 2.2 children, folklore.... Is only a suburb way, a cousin ora grandmother away. (315)

Karnad says,

> It needs to be stressed here that these tales are not left-overs from the past. (315)

G.K.Chesterton in his essay titled 'On Archeology' explains the petrifying effect of the past,

> We talk of the past as dead; but there is a very special and definite sense in which the past is always a living thing while the future is a dead thing. We know that the past has moved on living lines; but we can only conceive the future as moving on dead lines, the historic past is full of those free actions and frustrated prophecies... a man looking at the round arches of the old Roman and Norman architecture could not possibly have calculated from them that a hundred years afterwards, the delicate energy of the Gothic world be piercing the sky if we want the wildest emotions of novelty and astonishment, we can only find them in mouldering stores and folding tapesteries, in the museum of antiquities or the place of tombs. (11-15)

Lionet Trilling in his essay 'The Sense of the Past' says,

> The historical sense, that is to be understood as the critical sense, as the sense which life uses to test itself.... Mietzschis definition prescribes that culture be studied and judged as life's

> continuous evaluation of itself, the evaluation being understood as never finding full expression in the 'operating forces' of a culture, but as never finding full expression at all without reference to those gross institutional facts. (270-71)

It is very difficult to define human relationship and the factors which influence it: Is it nature around us? Is it culture that we inherit and continue ? Or is it something else which cannot be defined? This has been elaborated in the poems like 'Love Poem for a Wife and Her Trees' and 'Looking for the Centre'. It is but natural that physical reproduction occurs in the branches of "family trees", "with their roots in heaven/and branches in the earth", it confirms that man is inextricably bound to the cosmos. The nexus with nature is paradoxical and imminent and he explains it in the poem 'One Move on a Deathless Theme',

> Everyone in this street
> will became cold, like under stores
> or be scattred as ash In rivers and oceans.

And then came the term of time and culture forming the integral part of human life,

> Time moves in and out of me a stream of sound, a breeze, an
> electric current that seeks the ground....
> Morning brown into evenings before I turn around in the day.

For Ramanujan times is the cycle process of life which keeps on rotating all the time and stream of humanity keeps on going unstopped.

Ramanujan's poetry is replete with irony and in the words of Edward Said it is 'Worldly', coping with life as it is, rather an affirmation of it,

> Yet days can be golden,
> apples beautiful if eyes can see
> only days and apples. ('If eyes can be')

It has been felt that in Indian English poetry a process of declononization has taken place alongwith the political decolonization, Bruce King is of the view that it is a product of an independent nation and culture (110) but we may easily rebut his assertion because Indian English poetry came into life before Independence through it 'British root' cannot be denied. He is also wrong in his observation that this school of poetry 'seldom focus on local society and realities.' (110) Ramanujan's poetry evolve out of Indian experience and sexsibility which include 'its memories of family, local places, images, beliefs and history,' (115) often accused of being sceptical, ironical and unrealistic using conflict, argument and surprises. Even in the alien land his inherited Tamil Brahminism and south Indian culture does not betray him. Bruce King writes about his tools and techniques,

> The word play, puns, inner rthythems, rhetorical devices, ironies, distanced neutrality of tone, understatement, compression and elliptical progression the poems have similarities to his translations highly aware of the conventions, techniques and structures of Indian verse and these have been used and transformed in his English poetry. (116)

His poetry is not immunised from the flow of modernity as he had extensive study of Yeats and Eliot; consequently, his poetry revel "complexity, instability and irony" of the moderns, most often based on old Indian poetic conventions and medieval poetry of sages. He traces the elements of modern science in classical Indian writings, though he practised Buddhist meditation. As Bruce King says,

> Everything is unstable, changing, transitory, predatory, striving to survive. He welcomed modernity but his sensibility was shaped by a view of life as repetitive cycles which have the appearance of change. (299)

At times, his poetry seems to be highly personal. As a diasporic idol his poems illustrate the negotiations between cultures of the Indian and the alien and his role appears to be that of the hyphen between Indian and America (Indian-American). He is also taken as "the last major modernist, the poet of the perfect, concive, imagist lyric"(300). His poetry includes the influence of the modernists, and conventions of Tamil and Kannada poetics. In 'introduction' to The Black Hen' Dharwadker puts emphasis on the concern of Ramanujan with the body in relation to time and death. The black hen has an image suggestive of 'fertility and life' and its red eye is suggestive of anxiety and death,

> The black hen stares with its round eye and you're afraid.
> It is in response to the prevalent romantic aesthetic,
> it cames sometimes as the black hen with the red round eye.

Perhaps this is the repucursion of the Upanishadic wisdom that he had acquired through extensive study of *Vedas* and *Upnishadas* and we find it in the form of "poetic inspiration, anxieties and death" which is also said to be influence of the theory/vision of cause and effect, the cycle of life and death etc., the larger views of life,

> I hear it running like an underground
> Ganges under my feet,
> over my head....
> always running from me

In all existence, life and death are interwired and so for Ramanujan, every object has the potential to be studied. Later on he thought of propagating his ideas and revealed his philosophical vision with a deliberate inclusion of autobiographical ingredients which also comprise his treatment of life as a sexual desire, longings of the flesh, particularly of the days after divorce and continual longing for her and his family. It has been alleged that he acquaints us with "similar ideas, phrases or images" (303) and also carries the conventions of medieval Tamil poetry. He had many close friends but his domestic life was a failure and it affected the philosophical and psychological theme of his poetry. Vilas sarang is of the view that "Ramanujan's poetry springs out of deep inner compulsion, and is not merely the by-product of a well-trained scholarly mind. True, there is a certain inhibited quality about Ramanujan's poetry... the inner turmoil... pretentions,ambition...strewn with references, inner and physical violence derangement.... psychosis.... anxiety and despair... darkness enters...." (24-25)

He also says that "translation of poetry rather than writing of it, appears to have been Ramanujan's primary and more constant concern." (24) Yet we find some positive qualities in him, for instance the artistic control that he has over his disturbing flow of emotion which can never attain undue height; he has a measured and quiet tone, trim and tidy image, intricate and tight sentences and calculated passion. Family is his obsession which renders a nasty subjective outfit and exposes his limitations; and what we find is his son sitting in some corner, wife crying aloud, father lamenting for nothingness, mother carrying unabated affection, sister mad with zeal, cousin shouting for guidance, etc., in 'Ecology' his son is angry, in 'Routin Day Sonnet' his wife laments, and so on. His, 'Second Thought' is such a collection which tells us all about what he wants to communicate, that is, 'Fear', 'Pleasure', 'A Minor Sacrifice', 'Alien', 'Zoo Gardens Revisited', 'Son to Father to Son', 'At Forty', 'Middle Age', and 'Looking' and 'Finding'. K.R.S. Iyengar in his book *Indian Writing in English* quotes him as "the most talented of the 'new' poets". Moreover, Iyengar also signals at something else when he says,

> He has also used English with great simplicity and force in some of the *vachanas* from Karnad and some of the love lyrics from the *Kuruthohai*. These latter have won praise from Tamil and English scholars alike, and it is no small achievement to have matched the old sophistications of romantic love to the current sophistication of linguistic finish. (671)

He quotes,

> What kin is your mother to mine? What was my father to your anyway? And how did you and I meet ever? But our hearts are as red earth and pouring rain: mingled beyond panting.

Iyengar compares the crowd of 'The Striders' with the denizens of Dante's hell, the mutilated beggar, the drowned woman and their disturbing misery and agony, and then the poor Rickshawallah,

> His arms and legs were wholly literate: in green and in red the indelible names of friends long, dead.... The tattoo will stand, green, red when all else is gone.

Keeping in view his diasporic identity his *Relations* is more important because it reflect his maturity and serves as a bridge between his years in India and those in America. We have a taste of his bitterness in his reminiscence, "this little ounce of bitterness, this memory/This load that weight a thousand tones, and yet/is rich, bitter rich, because it is my life." Iyengar has called the essence of Ramanujan,

> Oh God, oh God, oh misgotten One!
> You fool, there is no promised land
> And then the mysterious man that he finds everywhere,

> I touched him.
> He was not there.
> He fled, laughing, weeping.
> Yet he was next to me.
> Where did he live?
> An hotel room.
> I asked him who he was.
> He said mockingly:
> Can't you guess? I am loneliness.

It is all in the seventeen pieces of Leslie de Noronha's 'Poem' whose last poem is most remarkable,

> That I must harbour the silent chalice of self-knowledge,
> Bitterly, profoundly
> My hatred a glorious requiem
> A hymn, a symphony...

M.K. Naik quotes him as "the most outstanding poet of the sisties... another exile." (199) To understand the constitution of the poetic sensibility and mental make-up of Ramanujan it is very important to take care of his own confession as quoted by R. Parthasarathy in his book *Ten Twentieth Century Indian Poets* (Delhi:1976, pp.95-96) and further quoted by M.K.Naik,

> English and my disciplines [linguistics, anthropology] give me my 'outer' forms—linguistic, metrical, logical and other such ways of shaping experience, and my thirty years in India, my frequent visits and field trips, my personal and professional preoccupations with Kannada, Tamil, the classes and folklore give me my substance, my 'inner' forms, images, symbols. (200)

Obviously, his poetry is burdened with his 'racial burden', 'Hindu heritage', 'Ancestral crocodiles and tortoise' and, no doubt, 'domestic upheavels'. Yet he is aware of the worth and imperfections, sustenance and limitations of these ethos. He holds in esteem its values in the poem 'Christmas' which celebrate the 'Vision of unity of all life',

leaf from parrot
Or branch from root
Nor... that tree from you or me.

He admits his mission as his weakness or limitation,

I must seek and will find
My particular hell in my Hindu mind.

After all, he is a modern Hindu and so he can trace the gap/rift between the traditional and modern Hindu entity explicit in his poems; his utterances are noteworthly,

The Hindoo: he reads his Gita and is calm at all events
The Hindoo: he doesn't Hunt a fly or spider either.

M.K.Naik says,

> His anticulation of the Hindu ethos has so far produced (with a few nitable exceptions) poetry of the periphery and not the centre of the Hindu experience. (202)
>
> A later poem like 'Prayers to Lord Murugan' even reveals a curious uncertainty in his reaction to Hinduism. Perhaps Ramanujan has yet to came fully to terms with his heritage and is still feeling his way. Meanwhile, he has effectively demonstrated to his contemporaries the supreme importance of having roots, and has also shown glimpses of the vitality the work of a poet acquires when he succeeds even partially in his attempt. (202)

KV. Surendran in his book *Indian English Poetry: New Perspective* writes,

> Panthasarthy has observed that the quality of experience he would like to express in English and the quality of the Indian he uses are the twin problems for an Indian writing in English. A.K. Ramanujan who can certainly be referred to as the poet

> of the Indian sensibility in one is able to easily and effortlessly survive both these problems. He successfully turned the ordinary into the exotic and the exotic into the ordinary. His poems are noted for their variety and the skilled use of the language. (710)

It is very important to note that the post-independence poetry suffers from a peculiar kind of vacuum after the departure of the British. As O. P. Bhatnagar point out,

> The end of slavery is the beginning of the freedom to be free. The sudden departure of the British from India made Indian confront a variety of anomalies, conflicts, contradictions and paradoxes welling up their subconscious, necessitating redefinition of their roles and commitments in the changed. Context of the times felt more keenly in Indian poetry in English. The most important dilemma the poets felt was one of alienation in their own land and therefore the paradox of belonging. (199)

Regarding A. K. Ramanujan he says,

> A.K. Ramanujan turned to history, tradition, myth, literature and family to contain the alienation of the self forced by his stay away from his roots, abroad. In him the modern mind came face to face with tension of having a 'home' back home, a man settled abroad.... In him the problems of life and poetry converge polishing images, irony and reflective skill...his Indian psyche and identity alive in a foreign land and also accept the plurality of identity. (210-11)

His disasporic identity provides an additional quality in asserting and analysing a situation, an individual or a mythology. He strides back objectively and approaches his personal concern most often to generalize and universalize it in a unique way, that is, the approach is Indian but the modality is Western, taken it other round while the selling is Western, the mode of observation is Indian; thus the first poem of *The Striders* (1966) has the image of New England water insect, the most effective poetic technique to convey his feeling,

And search
For certain thin-
stemmed, bubble-eyed water bugs.
See them pench
On dry capillary legs
Weightless
On the ripple skin
Of a stream

Not only prophets
Walk on water. This bug sits
On a landslide of lights
And dream eye-
Deep
Into its tiny strip
Of sky. ('Striders')

His two faculties of reasoning and sentiment from a balance and suggest a relationship which dictates his ideology and mission:

...Water is all eyes.
The earth has bone for muscle.
And the air is a flock of invincible pigeons.
But anxiety
Can find no metaphore to end it. ('Anxiety')

His endeavour is to define his own self, his own personality, his own being, and in order to do so he is a bit sceptic and philosophical:

I resemble everyone but myself,
and sometimes see
in shop windows despite the well-known laws
of optics
the portrait of stranger

date unknown
often signed in a corner
by my father (Self-portrait)

The inherited Hinduism and the sanskar torture him, and his poetic self is, most of the time, at war with the fanatic sensibilities with a pinch of ironic stance, and finally, there is the triumph of his poetic sensibility, and the impossible ideals of Hinduism is defected; consequently the incongruities and contradictions surface, for instance, the philosophy of detachment in Hinduism is both a riddle and the target of ridicule,

At the bottom of all this bottomless
enterprise to keep simple hearts gain beat
the only risk is heartlessness. ('The Hindoo', *The Only Risk*)

He reasons his memories as a detached critic and his emotional self lies flat against such irony trains of his poetic self,

Memory
in a crowd of memories, seems
to have no place
at all for unforgettable things
('On Memory', *The Striders*)

Such memories are inadequate tools to investigate the past, that' is, the convention, the tradition, the sanskar and the roots, which on the other hand, help him to discover and rediscover his own self; through this technique of self-discovery he discovers the vicinity, the universe and the whole mankind, so it is a journey from self-hood to the rest of the universe, a sort of globalisation of the self. This expression of the self also acquaints him with the strength and weakness of his own self and the entire humanity on the whole; it is his diasporic self which rebels against his conventional background,

I am lined
on branches bare as roots
Without that latest
hatch of births- bewildered parrots. ('Christmas')

Here, he serutinizes his own self and the situation is best brought out by a leafless free being watered by an Indian in the USA. His discovery is a continual process of research for the self to establish "a pattern of permanence in the flux/flow of personal experience turning poetry of reverie into the poetry of immediacy or authenticity, a kind of juxtaposition of the poetic experience of reality and the search for the self." (213) And so he discovers,

....I cannot unlearn
Conventions of despair
They have their pride
I must seek and will find
My particular hell only in my Hindu mind.
('Conventions of Despair', *The Striders*)

And his nostalgic earnestness resonates further way back, roll to past to locate the epicentre, the pivotal point,

Something opened
in the past and I heard something shut
in the future, quietly
Like the heavy door
of my mother's black pillared nineteenth century
Silent house, given on her marriage day
to my father, for a dowry.
('Still Another for Mother', *The Striders*)

In the poem 'Small Scale Reflection on a Great House', he is haunted by ideas instead of nostalgia, "And ideas behave like rumours, one casually mentions somewhere they came back to the door as prodigies born to a prodigal father with eyes that vaguely look our own."

Besides the Hinduism and its rituals, personal life and family, India and its way of life, Ramanujan lapsed into the spiritual world, the supreme power of Almighty and His abode, which we may call a positive force or a divine compulsion or a sort of enlightenment towards creative urge of life and towards the value under preservation and perceptions of their place in a man, family, society and the world at large, and so he says in 'A Poem on Particulars',

> I have heard it said
> among the planters
> you can sometimes count
> every orange
> on a tree
> but never
> all the trees
> in a single
> orange.

In the poem 'The Watchers', Ramanujan is obsessed with the truth as essence of life and the inability of the poet to convey us,

> Lighter than light, blowing like air
> through keyholes, they watch without questions
> the watchers,
> they watch even the questions as I live
> over and over with cancelled stamps
> on verandas.

Ramanujan's poetic self evolves to maturity in the poem 'Chicago Zen', in the process of self-exploration and discovery of one's own entity,

> Now you know what you always know;
> the country cannot be reached
> by jet. Nor by boat or jungle river
> ... ...
> but only by answering ordinary

> black telephones, questions
> walls and small children ask
> and answering all call of nature.

This is a sort of resolution that the poet makes in order to console himself and acquaint himself with the ongoings of the world, the flux of morality, humanity, values and the stance of the world.

Diverse cultural influences operate simultaneously in the making of a post-colonial and postmodern poet and his disasporic entity which we may call as an instance of polished, sophisticated and profound multiculturalism Ramanujan is such a poet and his poetry accommodates linguistic, literary and cultural features and farms of Tamil, Kannada and English literature. N. Sharada Iyengar in his paper 'The Portrait of an Antist' quotes Rama Jha's interview with Ramanujan which is relevant to quote here,

> One cannot live in the past, neither can you entirely live in the present, because we are not like that. The past never passes. Either the individual past, a historical past or a cultural past. It is with us, it is what gives us the richness... of understanding. And the richness of expression... creativity comes out of a sustained attention to one's own experience, one's own locality and one's own landscape you know. And the circumstances which one can feel and experience deeply without any scheme, without bearing this, that and other... whatever world it may be. It may be a personal world, it may be a social world, but a world which is fully embodied in poetry. We need enough of that, some part of our experience to explore it as best as we can. (124)

As an expatriate, Ramanujan lives in two worlds at once, one within and the one without, one Indian and the other western. Vasant A. Shahana and M. Sivarama Krishna in their paper titled 'Indian Poetry in English: A critical Assessment" says,

> Ramanujan and his contemporaries, Ezekiel and Kamala Das exhibit in their poetry three concentric circles of self in relation

> to society, self in relation to history with family as the core unit and self in relation to itself, its own propelled emotions and feelings. (127)

Modern British and American poets, particularly those of the post-war movement in poetry like Philip Lankin, Thomas Gunn, Elizabeth Jennings, etc., are indulged in exploring the meaning of existence through ordinary experience similarly the 'new poets' of Indian English writing are engrossed in writing the poetry of concrete experiences of men living in the modern world; consequently, their poetry is simple in theme and complex in image. S. Nagarajan explains it as follows,

> It is here that their poetry becomes a walk barefoot into reality and effacement of the ego. The concrete for them invariably carries the aroma of the private life of the experiencing self. They are mostly concerned with themselves and the surroundings allied to them. Their poetry records the artist's own life-history and his struggle against himself. (2)

Ramanujan's poetry falls in this category and it represents the common features of modern poetry such as variety of mood, tone and technical strategy. He is also taken to be a provincial poet like Philip Lankin. He has coined new images to shape his experiences of the truth of life, full of potential and prude; his poem 'Two Days' reveals the wheel of life caught in the flux of time.

Taken as a whole Ramanujan's poetry is an outstanding amalgamation—his experience of the bitter truth of life, his deep attachment with his family members, his inherited Hindu sentiments, pull of his knowledge of mythology both Tamil and Kannada and the fascination of the West—all treated with intellectual insight of a diasporic torn self.

References

Bhatanagar, O.P., 2002, "Poetry as Discovery", in *Studies in Indian Poetry in English*, (ed.) A.N.Prasad & U.S.Rukhaiyar, New Delhi: Sarup & Sons Pub.

Chesterton,G.K., 1995, *On Archeology, in English Prose & Poetry Selection*, Gauhati University, University Publication Department.

Dharwadker, A.B., 2008, *Collected Plays* (Vol. II), New Delhi: O.U.R.

Iyengar, KR.S., 2003, *Indian Writing in English*, New Delhi: Sterling Pub.

Iyer, N.S., 2002, "The Portrait of an Artist", in *Studies in Indian Poetry in English*, (ed.), A.N.Prasad & U.S.Rukhaiyar, New Delhi: Sarup & Sons Pub.

King, Bruce, 2001, *Modern Indian Poetry in English*, New Delhi: O.U.P.

Kumar, Shiv K., 1992, *Contemporary Indian Literature in English*, Shimla: I.A,S.

Nagarajan, S., 1977, *Contemporary Indian Poetry in English*, (ed.), Saleem Peeradina, Madras: MacMillan.

Naik, M.K., 1999, *A History of Indian English Literature*, New Delhi: Sahitya Akademi.

Naik, M.K., 2006, *Indian English Poetry: From the beginning upto 2000*, Delhi: Pencraft.

Sarang, Vilas, 1989, *Indian English Poetry since 1950: An Anthology*, Mumbai: Orient Longman.

Surendran, K.V., 2002, *Indian English Poetry*, New Delhi: Sarup & Sons Pub.

Trilling, Lionel, 2005, *The Sense of the Past, in Literary Criticism: A Reading*, (ed.), B.B.Das & J.M.Moharity, New Delhi: O.U.P.

Vasant A. Shahana and M. Sivarama Krishna, (ed.) 1980, *Indian Poetry in English: A Critical Assessment*, Delhi: Macmillan.

5

Loneliness: An Intrinsic Design of Wordsworth

Wordsworth is unlikeably liked by everyone. New Zealand born writer Fleur Addock remarks, "People talk about him as if he died yesterday" (*The Hindu*, October 10, 2004). A visit to the Wordsworth drives us to stumble upon his sagacious wasteland, misconstrued as somber divulgence of Nature. The present paper ventures to identify such hysterical junctures, trying to locate its justification, expounding his potential table.

A child of French Revolution, Wordsworth insisted for freedom of man and that too in everyman's colloquial language. Primarily a nature poet, he remains an informal puritan throughout his work. His output lays in bare his taste fashioned by contemporary setting. However, he claims to be more obliged to Nature and hence his response is more questionable.

Loneliness is something that deters the present generation. In American literature loneliness is felt everywhere, the question of identity assails and the problem of belongingness speaks aloud.

It should have been strange to the Romantics, though it is not so. Wordsworth's *Tintern Abbey* has sufficient evidence of his solitude:

> Once again
> Do I behold these steep and lofty cliffs

That on a wild secluded scene impress
Thoughts of more deep seclusion
....
....
But oft, in lonely rooms, and 'mid the din
Of town's and cities
of the deep rivers, and the lonely streams
Wherever nature led—more like a man
....
....
Therefore let the moon
Shine on thee in thy solitary walk
....
....
If solitude, or fear, or pain, or grief
Should be thy portions (II, 14-25)

The same resonance is there in 'The Recluse',

On Man, on Nature, and on Human life
Musing in solitude, I oft perceive
....
....
I, long before the blissful hour arrives
Would chant, in lonely peace, the spousal verse
Ripe solitary anguish, or must hang (II, 1-23)

Solitude implies segregation from society and concentration on self; on the other hand it also implies rejection by the society and the consequent seclusion. Grief, frustration, anguish, seclusion, perplexity and feeling of inconvenience with the world is the natural outcome of such a sick mental condition. Now the question is: who should be blamed—the society or the individual? Whatever the case may be, such complexity leads to individuality, seclusion and self-confinement. Repulsion from the outer world compels a prolong meditation, culminating in internal exploration and purgation; this is a same approach to serenity, penance and redemption. Another interpretation convinces us of the negation of the rest of the world which is a negative development and results in nihilism. Where is Wordsworth, a nihilist defying all existing fabrication or a formulator or salvation in his solitude? Or is it an appetite to resurrect himself divorcing the rest of Romantics? Or is it discontent with the inadequate and urge for perfection, perhaps, through transformation abandoning the hassles of life and taking the shelter of abundance of Nature? Talking of 'The Solitary Reaper' is a sane device to illustrate musicality of some unknown song and it appears to be a deliberate attempt of the bard to elicit the essence possible in seclusion only, and hence her being alone is imperative. But it seems to be out of context/proportion to move, "lonely as a cloud", "thoughts of more deep seclusion", "lonely rooms", "lonely streams like a man", "solitary walk", "musing in solitude", "solitary anguish", etc. "Lonely rooms" signifies the loneliness of metropolis and also the sick—pattern of the bard and his cynical being but why the search for isolation in the heavily crowded Nature? It is here that Wordsworth appears to be unconvincing. Why does it plague him so often? Is it same intrinsic design of the bard that comes through his poetic eloquence?

Perhaps the answer lies in 'Preface to *the Lyrical Ballads* where Wordsworth makes it clear,

> ... our continued influxes of feelings are modified and directed by out thoughts which are indeed the representatives of all our past feelings; and... by contemplating the relation of these general representatives to each other, we discover what is really important to men. (127)

This is how Wordsworth defines the process of writing poetry for which he felt the need of meditation. By following the fluxes and refluxes of the mind in a state of excitement the poem results and for Wordsworth, the feeling and thinking go simultaneously.

In 'Lines Written a Few Miles Above Tintern Abbey', a powerful poem of self-expression, stating Wordsworth's creed, is distinguished by alteration between assertion and doubt, regulating the structural dynamics. Wordsworth elaborates the role of nature in the life of man and the steps in the development of the human mind; Dorothy serves the link between the poet and nature. He travels within himself, to an observation of his own mind as being representative of the general through observation of the rustic as the prototype, consequently reflecting the universal. With 'a sad perplexity', an uncertainty looms large over the description of the landscape,

> Once again I see
> There hedge-rows, hardly hedge rows, little lines
> Of sportive wood run wild
> and wreaths of smoke
> Sent up in silence, from among the trees
> With some uncertain notice, as might seem
> Of vagrant dwellers in the houseless woods.

As the poem proceeds we find a note of hesitation. The curve of ascent towards mystical affirmation is counter-balanced a bit ahead: "If this/Be but a vain belief, yet, oh!" (11,49-50) Here Wordsworth is not confident in his assertion and his mystical apprehension of the relation between man and nature and so it takes the form of a vain belief'. He is cautious in returning to the aspect of his experience of which he is more assured, offering a personal testimony to the sustaining and restorative power of nature in the disturbed moments of life. We may notice, a similar alternation between supreme assertion and doubt as we proceed ahead in the mainstream of the poem. The role of nature in his own development is remarkable, and he admits it,

> In nature and the language of the sense
> The anchor of my purest thoughts, the nurse

> The guide, the guardian of my heart, and soul
> Of all moral being. (II, 109-112)

Subsequently, the 'Wye Valley' becomes representative of the world of nature in general; the 'green valley' is transformed into the 'green earth'; the world of the 'eye' and the 'ear' becomes 'mighty world'; the microcosm widens out to become the macrocosm; the general in the external world of nature is reached through a particular microcosmic landscape. The mental world of the poet faces transition at par with the external world, and finally the personal testimony of the poet is corroborated and universalized, and yet the whole poem oscillates between doubt and assertion.

Wordsworth's other poems such as 'The Recluse', 'The Excursion', 'Resolution and Independence' etc., affirm his flexibility between the personal and the general. He explains it in his own way:

> I describe myself as having been exalted to the highest pitch of delight by the joyousness and beauty of nature; and then as depressed, even in the midst of those beautiful objects to the lowest dejection and despair. (70)

That is why he switches to the other extreme of dejection and despair. He again elaborates himself:

> My whole life I have lived in pleasant thought,
> As if life's business were a summer mood;
> As if all needful things would come unsought
> To genial faith, still rich in genial good. (II, 36-39)

Here, Wordsworth answers to the poet's dejection and despair. This happens because the poets tend to live away from reality. He further says: "We poets in our youth begin in gladness;/But there of come in the end despondency and madness." (11,48.49)

Obviously this is a common problem for poets with a profound imagination.

It is for this reason that his 'Leech Gatherer' swings between acceptance and hesitation, individual and general, singular earthly existence and a visionary stature, and finally the 'bent double' old man transcends the barrier of time and space, and seems to move like a Christ-like figure, a living embodiment of pursuance not just for Wordsworth, Coleridge, Chattertan or Burns, but for all imaginative souls of all time and place, though "wandering about alone silently." (131) After the usual binary opposition between assertion and doubt, comes universalization and acceptance. This is a subjective solution, a personal testimony of the poet and a personal answer to despondency in the form of the old man.

'The Excursion' is another poem where the interaction of four characters, that is, the Wanderer, the Solitary, the Pastor, and the Narrator, manifest Wordsworth's contradictory aspects of personality. The Wanderer is the possible Wordsworth, the Solitary is the sceptic poet, the Pastor is the Church poet and the Narrator, the objective observer. The Wanderer and the Solitary establish the functional binary opposition in the structures of the poem. The Solitary suits our purpose, he is prompted to come out of his cave—like abode, confront the sun and understand the essence of life which is not just unhappiness and despondency. The debate between the Wanderer and the Solitary is remarkable. The Wanderer looks at the sustaining features of life and the Solitary questions the values of life.

The debate remains inconclusive and then arrives the Pastor with a Christian answer to despondency but fails; the contradiction continues. The riddles that assail the Solitary are:

i) Is man a child of hope?

ii) Do generations of man continue without progress?

iii) Is man stopped by death without reaching his destination or without finding an answer?

iv) What dominates in man—good or evil?

v) What preoccupies man—reason or heart?

vi) What is virtue—power, beauty, health or something else?

vii) Are we doomed to decay and expire in dust?

These issues cause the Solitary's dejection; the Pastor is invited to provide an answer with his abstract reasonings and Christian tenets and tales of life lived in actuality. By the end of the day, the Solitary is completely transformed:

> "Another sun"
> Said he, "shall shine upon us ere we part
> Another sun, and per adventure more" (Bk IX, 11, 779-81)

Unargumentatively issues raised by the Solitary, that is, the voice of the poet within, he finds answers in universalizing the problem, shifting from 'I' to 'we'. He runs from mundane understanding to religious persuasions, from individual ethos to Christian ethics, from personal complicacy to general suffering but he fails miserably to infer, and remains inconclusive. This antagonism of Wordsworth's inner self continues throughout his work and remains unanswered. It is the dramatization of intricate relationship between the mind of man, the world of nature and human experience in all its complex beauty. His excursion, both internal and external, is a quest to identify what is not and yet mistaken; and his anguish, an outcome of the "fever of the world" pervades throughout his work as "The World is too much with us."

A similar voice is audible in one of the songs of Bengal,

Dekhechi rupsagrey maner inanush Kancha sona
Tarey dhari dhaari money karl, dhorteygeley dhara dey na

(In the ocean of beauty I have discovered the person within,
the pure gold
I tried to catch hold of him but he remained unknown to me.)

References

Owens, W.J.B. and Smyser, J.W., (eds.), 1974, *The Prose Works of William Wordsworth*. London: OUP.

Selincourt, E. De and Davbishire, H. (eds.), 1974, *The Poetical Works of William Wordsworth*. London: OUP.

6

Keats's Positive Religiosity: A Probe into His Artistic Integrity

Keats has been positive: in his melancholy, in his brooding and even in his suffering. This has become almost his religion that sustains his entire work as a positive inflow available in the progression of his making. The present paper aims to examine his work in order to locate such strings that constitute his artistic being.

Let us start with *Ode to a Nightingale* that brings about a state of near extinction, undergoes extinction and finally the primary victim, the poet's self, resurfaces as resurrection. The poem evolves out of the simultaneous ventures of the two: the nightingale in its undefined natural outflow and the poet under threat of annihilation in his continual yielding. Her song creeps into Keats's heart nearly paralysing his own identity. He experiences "pain of bliss" and "drowsy numbness" assails him, contaminating his whole constitution; "the centre cannot hold" and the poet is all helpless, "as though of hemlock I had drunk/ or emptied some dull opiate to the drains/one minute past, and lethe-wards had sunk", it is as if "a draught of vintage" consumed—yet it is not sickening rather sinking towards oblivion, releasing him from the world:

> from Fade far away, dissolve, and quite forget
> ....

> The weariness, the fever, and the fret
> Here, where men sit and hear each other groan
> ....
> Where but to think is to be full of sorrow
> Away! Away! For fly to thee

Keats is lost, completely submerged in the bird's over-powering song, united like two yearning age-old lovers, almost blinded:

> I cannot see what flowers are at my feet
> Nor what soft incense hangs upon the boughs

Followed by...

> ...in love with easeful Death
> ....
> To cease upon the midnight with no pain,
> ....
> In such an ecstasy!
> drifting towards immortality.

All of a sudden, he is taken aback, the bell tolls for him the process of disillusionment initiates and thereby starts self-questioning:

> Was it a vision, or a waking dream?
> Fled is that music:-Do I wake or sleep?

Keats's back journey is a sort of revival, a new lease of life, acceptance of the life as it is of "groan", "think", "sorrow", "despair", and "pain"

> Where palsy shakes a few, sad, last gray hairs,
> Where youths grows pale, and spectre-thin and dies.

It is here that he realizes,

> The fancy cannot cheat so well
> As she is famed to do, deceiving elf.

The concluding part of *Ode to a Nightingale* reaffirms his belief in the present, in the life that he has and not in the romantic imaginary world—a world of illusion. And here lies the positivity of Keats, religiosity of Keats and his essentiality. And it is here that he surpasses all the Romantics, in his ultimate choice of death-in-life character of the world.

Keats's bird emerges as a gigantic influence like Shaw's Morell, pervades thoroughly but is not devoid of erosion. As a consequence, like Morell it dissolves into nothingness whereas the weak poet surrenders completely, regains his lost consciousness, not to be kicked out of the scenario but to persist, to face the world as it is. Keats's letters make his intention clearer where he says,

> This is the world—thus we cannot expect to give away many hours to pleasure..... circumstances are like clouds continually gathering and bursting—while we are laughing the seed of some trouble is put into the wide arable land of events...

Obviously, pleasure is not life and escape from its hardship is not the solution. And so he says in "Lines Written in the Highlands After a Visit to Burns' Country" that if one remains "Beyond the sweet and bitter world" he may turn insane and that a overstay there might "bar return" and he decides not to forget the "remembered face" and not to "lose his mind on mountains black and bare", for he must keep "his vision clear from speak, his inward sight unblind."

This is the poet's hard-earned wisdom, a sublimation of self-education and his poetics, a combination of the two: departure from the real to the unreal and then a return to the here and now of work-a-day self; his poetry is the blending of these movements. In *Ode to a Nightingale* the poet takes imagination ('fancy') as a "deceiving self", creative of illusions both sedative and intoxicant but he clearly disfavours their prolonged effects in-as-much-as they fall short of real fulfilment and only leave us at the end to unbearable forlorns, to obliterate the non-poetic. In "The Fall of Hyperion" Moneta, the High Priestess accuses and advises the poet-narrator,

> Thou art a dreaming thing
> A fever of thyself-think of earth

Moneta suggests to tame the "feverish, sensation mongering, enchantment-loving and self-gratifying imagination" by embracing reality of suffering which may serve as a prelude to the realization of the poet's greatest powers, and this is a sort of self-suggestion to the poet himself as he feels "Every sole man hath days of joy and pain." He enjoys his 'sickness' that is medicinal but not ignoble" and now he is:

> a sage/A humanist, physician to all men

Moneta defines the role of a poet as that of a creator of anodyne, to lessen suffering and not to vex the world with dreams. He must see as a god sees and to apply mental faculties in presenting anything, and this is his strength:

> Such things as thou art admitted oft
> Into like gardens than didn't pass erewhile.
> And suffered in these temple: for that cause
> Thou standest safe beneath this statue's knees.

In general, romanticism stands for the same, a explained by Prof. Amaresh Dutta,

> Philosophically it represents a search for the inner truth hidden beneath the heaps of appearance, politically a kind of radicalism, a revolt against the establishment aesthetically an ecstatic and inspirational quest for the unattainable, or an

> ethereal idealisation of reality, and negatively and in extreme terms day-dreaming or a quixotic changing of the wind-mill. In any case, it articulated eternal propensity of the human mind and calls into being what is supposed to be its antipode—the classical epitomizing another aspect of human psyche, the two forming the duality of the Dionysiac and the Apollonian. (D.U. JES No. 12, 1996-97)

Keats's poetics involves striving and searching for all such "giant agony of the world" and "labour for moral good" "like slave to poor humanity" and "seek no wonder but the human face." Keatsean insight implies pain and suffering as an intrinsic pattern of human life that constitutes the integrity or purity of vision.

Ode on a Grecian Urn is another instance of Keats's commitment taken to be, a definitive aesthetic statement reflecting on human life in general, establishing beauty as the only worthwhile thing to be aspired. Here the vision of life is vibrant and organic that evolves out of paradox and contraries of diverse nature: temporal and eternal, conviction and truth, joy and sorrow, knowledge and ascension, mysterious and speculative, tragic and educative, cool and disturbing, and, imaginative and rationale. The poem opens with his dismissal of history and preference for legends as his usual practice in 'Endymion', 'The Eves of St. Agnes', 'The Fall of Hyperion', etc. History being the record of external things is liable to be rejected whereas legend embodies the stirrings and urges of the human heart and spirit that remain unchanged throughout the ages and help us to discover ourselves. Here the dichotomy of history and legend does not persist, rather they merge into each other with a new kinship to enact "haunting about thy shape, indistinguishably men or gods." From this paradox, Keats derives the soul of art as an invitation to the spirit, the victory of timelessness over time, the lover's passion to hold and kiss and yet fail to consummate his desire,

> Bold lover, never, never can't thou kiss,
> Though winning near the goal yet, do not grieve
> She cannot fade
> Forever wilt thou love, and she, be fair.

In totality, a lover never achieves his goal "though winning near the goal." Keats humanises the picture of the urn and brings us closer to the hearts of men in the midst of an eternal proximity. Love is, .

> Forever warm and still to be enjoyed,
> Forever panting, and forever young,
> All breathing human passion far above,
> That leaves a heart sorrowful and cloyed,
> A burning forehead, and a parching tongue

Love, passion, beauty and truth are timeless representing eternity,

> When old age shall this generation waste,
> Thou shall remain, in midst of other woe,

The poet who begins with projecting the urn as "unravished bride of quietness" and "foster child of silence and slow time", questions its features, its history, its legend visiting Tempe and 'Arcady', the places of beauty and 'wild ecstasy', foresees the alien future, "Heard melodies are sweet, but those unheard/Are sweeter...". This is a 'mad pursuit', a 'struggle to escape', an endless chase with a meaningful conclusion.

> She cannot fade, though thou hast not thy bliss
> Forever will thou love, and she be fair!

And in this land of beauty, spring is timeless, melody is timeless, joy is timeless, desire is timeless, youth is timeless and passion is timeless. Then follows the melancholy of desolation after 'sacrifice' and that of "marble men and maidens wrought with forest branches and the trodden weed" creeping into silence. Keats establishes,

> Beauty is truth, truth beauty—that is all
> Ye know on earth, and ye need to know.

The 'nightingale' is a victim of illusion but the 'urn' is a pursuit that finally establishes the timelessness of beauty which cannot fade and 'be fair' 'forever', the philosophy of life that led Keats throughout his life and work.

In the 'Grecian Urn', the poet is sorrow-conscious and hence a "friend to men", integrated into life; in his other odes, like, 'Ode to Apollo', 'Hymn to Apollo', 'Ode to May', 'Ode On Indolence', and 'Ode to Fanny', the question of poetry props up, poetic self is interrogated, poet's pursuit seems to be threatened and the poet's destination is calculated. Keats's desire for indolence torments the poet in 'Ode to Fanny', and he speaks out: "O ease my heart of verse and let me rest" and later on "A theme! a theme! great nature! Give a theme". It is a cry of the self-torments of jealousy. 'Ode on Indolence' refers to the state of indolence in which love, poetry and ambitions are reduced, to phantoms which can be diluted. 'Ode to May', 'Hymn' to Apollo' and 'Ode to Apollo' illustrate the problems of poetry. In fact, he wanted to present melancholy as a relieving force from the suffering caused by unbearable grief and tormenting jealousy, relevant for all men and women but in his personal case it proved to be a meaningless exercise for his failing health. Thus he embraces the actualities of the human life, a sustaining force and not a negative one; his wish to be near Fanny and the wisdom of keeping away from her seems to be parallel to the wish to continue to be a poet and the wisdom of temporality, ceasing to be so. Keats is anxious of the social utility of a poem and the role of the poet shaped accordingly, as he speaks out in 'To My Brother George',

But what, without the social thought of thee,
would be the wonders of the sky and sea?

Sonnet 14 is remarkable in the sense that the poet shifts from flowers and wonders to "The social smile, the chain for freedoms sake" and reaffirms that the hum/Of mighty workings" will give the world "another heart/and other pulses." In sonnet 15, the poet admits, "the poetry of earth is never dead" that results in "tremendous birth/to a loud hymn", and thus proceeds on its social role. Keats has decided not to be deceived by 'fancy'.

No, never more,
Shall airy voices cheat me to the shore
Of tangled wonder, breathless and aghast.

The poet has realised the sinister character of the imagination, dwelling on the meretricious charm of things, like the monstrous swell of visionary seas, the airy voices, and the cloudy phantasms—all far away from man's "natural sphere", as he reveals in 'Endymion',

There never lived a mortal man, who bent
His appetite beyond his natural sphere,
But starv'd and died gone and past
Are cloudy phantasms,
Caverns lone, farewell,
And air of visions, and the monstrous swell
Of visionary seas.

As an "arbitrary queen of senses" fancy has a profound influence on the poet and he confesses,

she took me like a child of suckling time,
and cradled me in roses.

In 'La Belle Dame Sans Merci', the knight is the victim who cries out,

I saw pale kings, and princes too
Pale warriors, death-pale were they all:
Who cry'd—La Belle Dame Sans Merci
Hath thee in thrall

Keats suggests a fearful aesthetic possibility of being victimized by a false, illegitimate fancy in one's unconsciousness. In 'The Poet' he is highly democratic and defines the social aspects of poetry, to assimilate all animate and inanimate, to be master of one's mother tongue that is a social aspect of poetry to assimilate all animate and inanimate, to be master of one's mother tongue that is a social instrument of fellowship, to suspect one's own identity, and thus serve a social purpose. His philosophy seems to be destructive of poetic imagination in 'Lamia', where "all charms" seem to perish "at the mere touch of cold philosophy" and "clip an angel's wings" and, further, the same philosophy is responsible to,

Conquer all mysteries by rule and line
Empty the haunted air, and ground mine
Unweave a rainbow.

We find a similar experience in 'Sleep and Poetry' where he bids goodbye to enslaving enchantment,

All that was for human senses fitted
....
Yes, I must pass them for a nobler
Where I may find the agonies, the strife
Of human hearts
....
A sense of real things comes doubly strong
And like a sudden stream, would bear along
My soul to nothingness: but I will strive
Against all doublings, and will keep alive

Most of the time, we feel that Keats is hovering between his two worlds: imaginative and realistic; his imagination continually impelled him to meditate on poetry, and these meditations have the same ideas and insights that we find in his poetics constructed out of his letters and other writings, reflecting his conviction earned out of endless self-education, Yet he prefers to dwell back on the 'world' itself,

> The common cognomen of this world among the misguided and superstitions is 'a vale of tears' from which we are to be redeemed by a certain arbitrary interposition of God and taken to Heaven—what a little circumscribed straightened national Call the world if you please 'the vale of soul making'. Then you will find out the use of the world....

His letters tell us about the unpredictably hostile circumstances of the nature of existence, and pain and suffering as intrinsic to life that constitute the necessary condition of acquiring integrity or purity of vision, and so he utters,

> Do you not see how necessary a world of pains and troubles is to school an intelligence and make It a soul? A place where the heart must feel and suffer in a thousand diverse ways.

For Keats, pain is educative; he is profoundly positive, holding the adversaries of life as indispensably flexible and formative, that provided authenticity to the artistic representation of man and his creativity, that is, art; each major or memorable persona of Keats shares the same experience, such as, Apollo, Endymion, Cynthia, Mnemosyne, Moneta, the Grecian Urn, Psyche and Cupid, Lamia and Lycius, Isabella, Lorenzo: the eternity glimpsed in the 'Grecian Urn' provides a stable vision, a complete and final affirmation of an immutable presence cognisant of human sorrow, expounding the mystery of truth and beauty, and investing life with a new significance. The vision is, invariably, that of a friend and benefactor, as made clear in' 'The Grecian Urn',

Thou shalt remain, in midst of the other woe
Than ours, a friend to man, to whom thou say'st
Beauty is Truth, truth-beauty that is all
Ye know on earth, and all ye need to know.

'The Grecian Urn' is directly related to the human world, and depicts man with his distinctive and wide-ranging concern, conceived in relation to nature, and in terms of his emotional, aesthetic and religious life. With its flora and fauna of nature as his immediate surrounding, man loses himself in his female counterpart and subsequently derives sustenance from nature; diverse manifestations of human situation allows man to know 'woe'—this is the intense awareness of the poet, that of melancholy; proximity and dissatisfaction, bereavement and togetherness, death and timelessness, eternity and brooding, endemic and pervasive that move together as compulsive adhesive feature of life, a redemptive measure for the entire mankind. And here lies the positive religiosity of Keats.

His artistic integrity implies his endeavour to strike a balance between the two, that is his imaginative flight and his realistic awareness, both poles apart; it is reflected throughout his poetry and it appears that he fails to escape his tendency of indulging 'fancy', accompanied by his passion for the truth, otherwise termed as "interchange of opposites," a struggle between the two worlds, inward and outward, of being and becoming, of past and future, intervened by the yearnings of the present—a clue to completeness of man. His poetic talent may have the bearings of his personal life: his birth, upbringing, education, profession etc; and his poetics, nothing but a sort of self-discovery, self-educative and personal workmanship. The sense of reality is fatal to his constitution as he feels, in 'Sleep and Poetry",

A sense of real things comes doubly strong
And like a sudden stream, would bear along
My soul to nothingness.

He is aware of the negative powers of reality, and says in the same poem:

> Is there so small a range
> In the present strength of manhood, that the high
> Imagination cannot fly.

He is of the firm view that it is imagination only that "soothe the cares, and lift the thoughts of man". He is between sensation and thought poetry and philosophy, real and unreal, and so in 'Lamia', "All charms fly/At the mere touch of cold philosophy" and can "clip an angel's wings". It is further made clear in 'Epistle to John Hamilton Reynolds,' where he admits, "High reason, and the love of good and evil" and asserts that imagination can be "Lost in a sort of Purgatory blind". In the sonnet 'To Spenser' Keats learns from the flower and says that wisdom "must drink the nature of the soil/Before it can put forth its blossoming."

Precisely Keats's poetry is a beautiful presentation of the mingling of the two, that is, imagination and reality: imagination as an adequate weapon to reach the tragic vision of the world; perhaps, like all Romantic poets, he thinks of himself as a philosophical and poetical revolutionary overthrowing the false gods and taste of the Age of Reason, as Blake says,

> To see a World in a Grain of Sand
> And the Heaven in a Wild Flower
> Hold Infinity in the palm of your hand
> And eternity in an hour.

Keats's artistic integrity involves his dwellings on the two opposites and his ability to blend them and present in a coherent way.

References

Abrams, M. H., (ed.), 1960, *A Note on Ode to a Nightingale*, London.

Bentley, G.E. 1977, *William Blacke's Writings*, Clarendon Press.

Blunden, E. (ed.), 1966, *Selected Poems: John Keats*, Collings, London.

Bush, D. 1937, *Mythology and the Romantic Tradition in English Poetry*, Cambridge, Mass.

Everet, W. 1965, *Aesthetic & Myth in the Poetry of Keats*, Princeton University Press.

Matthews, G.M., ed., (ed.), *Keats: The Critical Heritage*", Vikas Pub, New Delhi.

Rindley, M.R., 1964, *Keats' Craftsmanship*, Mathew Paperbacks.

Rollings, H.E., (ed.), 1958, *The Letters of John Keats. Cambridge*, Mass.

7

Bibhu Padhi's Poetry: A Chimerical Post-Colonial Offshoot

My first acquaintance with Bibhu Padhi as Indian English poet is from *Indian Literature* (vol. 230), where I found his four poems. I found him a different poet, and then I started my search for his book of poems and got one titled *Painting the House* of Disha Books, published long back in 1995. Later on I could come across his other books. His is an old signature, most legible and yet oblivious to most of us. Yet in the crowd of poets, he stands as a humble-chilled stature to be reckoned repeatedly, to be visited, revisited, and revisited—a fathomless depth of genuinity and relevance. This paper is to examine his poetry as a post-colonial offshoot of intense imaginary pursuit, an outburst of a dormant voice kept silent for long.

So far he has published these books of poems: *Going to Temple*, *A Wound Elsewhere*, *Lines from a Legend*, *Painting the House*, and *Games the Heart must Play*, touching almost all possible chords to dive deep within us. He is 'far from everybody, everything', mingling different tissues of felt experiences by grafting, mutation, and genetic engineering. The first striking point is his incessant waiting for someone, something, somewhere, unseen and unknown, for instance, "waiting to be back again" ('Of Hiding Important Things'), "we wait, but nothing shows" ('A Sense of Place'), "there's a sense of waiting", "long, night of waiting" ('Portrait of a Family'), "waiting for a different rain" ('Paper Town'), "we wait but this they know", "we wait for another season" ('Kites'), "we've been waiting for" ('Two Portraits by D. H. Lawrence'), "waiting for oxygenated", "waiting for since then waiting for the countless failures" ('The Burnt Town'), "waiting for its childish pranks too"('Acquaintance with Fire'), "the years that lie in wait—waiting for someone to take it up—the fascination of waiting"('Crossing Over'),"a love tree waiting" (The Farther Shore'), "the waiting days—sleep and wait" ('Dreaming Among Autumn Insects,), "waiting to greet me" ('Home'), "now waiting for its conclusion" ('Something Else'), "merely wait for" ('A Different Picture'), "our waiting skin to take it in" ('The Return of the Evening'), "approaching our waiting ears—wait for afternoon"('Drumbeats in the Afternoon'), "I've waited for yet other things to sail" ('Yet Another Year'), "I've only added to your waiting" ('Small Askings'), etc. And it continues unabated.

Jaydeep Sarangi is of the opinion that,

> A strange sense of loss pervades Padhi's poems. Inward- looking and at the same time deeply rooted in cultural and interpersonal realities, his poems speak to us in their own beguilingly simple language. (79)

The sense of culture is deeply rooted in his poems, be it the festivities, the luring beauty of religious and historical places, the temples, a family, the playing children in the afternoon, towards his son, or anything else. He is dead sure of its everlasting impact and its intense and wide influence in the poem 'Diwali',

> You could be here, there, anywhere,
> But the sounds and colours won't let you escape,
> The lights will find you out from the dark at last (7)

And while praying the goddess, he is left awestruck in the poem 'In the Temple',

> What if it is only a test–
> Of my willingness to accept defeat?
> Although I've decided to stand
> Here, my words drifting sluggishly
> In the strangant air, until they reach
> Her threshold of innocence and familiarity.(6)

And questions in 'Konark',

> Who shall hear my words, except
> The silences deep within stones?
> From these chance meetings, what
> Reward, what lost glory drifts in the air? (44)

As a stranger he talks to his son in the poem 'Poem for My Son',

> I seem to know all about you:
> Your time, your place, your name,
> The clean Indian—wheat colour
> Of your skin, your unpolished words. (4)

And in 'Portrait of a Family',

> You built this home and I only wish
> You had lived a little longer to see
> How, after you, it broke and crumbled–
> In spite of me, in spite of me. (32)

This is the lamentation over disintegration of the family today; the Oriental style of togetherness and the Occidental way of individuality, self-centredness, nuclearity and strangeness, how a son or father fails to recognise each other and how a family shatters.

The small children defy the mid-day sun and the poet forgets his late-afternoon sleep and peeps out to find,

The streets look empty, barren almost,
The town is without any other sound,
As if disowning everything except
These small children playing in dust. (3)

And then comes the rain, a good omen:

Dream of green fields
Return from the northern valleys,
From just under the Himalayas. (3)

The poet unveils the present world as it is, tries to locate it and tell us how we struggle with ourselves in our sleep, in midnight, in the darkness, in the city, among the ruins, in the fire, in the home, and other places:

And so we seek our proper sleep elsewhere,
beyond the closely linked nights and days, while
He continues to dance in his exotic outfit of smiles,
Plays on us his shrewd tricks of wakefulness. (10)

In the midnight he seeks consoling and asks for nothing,

Our bodies.
Are half dreaming till, while
Our generous words issue from
A place far within this night. (16)

In the deluge of humanity he finds himself all alone, somehow exiled in the roaring city, an intense feeling of isolation,

You are the exiled one.
No one listens to your words
....
....
And then, at the end of it all,
The long, cryptic silence of your
Own words madly rushing back at you. (23)

The poet tries to locate something but he fails,

> We wait, but nothing shows that might've recalled
> In a clear way a breath lost among night and time (27)
> ....
> ....
> What hope is still alive that might
> Carry us towards the desired place? (27)

When he reaches there, he finds it in a complete mess,

> I went in; he was right, perfectly so
> His good friends were trying desperately
> To retrieve the town from a terrible mess. (34)

The house for him is a different kind of dream,

> You must know that it requires
> A very different kind of dreaming
> Than any that you've known in the past
> ....
> ....
> The ancient dream
> That is shy to arrive, afraid of a past
> That could be too far away to be
> Recognised and owned. (47-48)

And the poet finally accepts,

> Home is where we are, today,
> This early morning hour. (63)

As we know post-colonialism could create the possibility of developing the poetics of double or multiple existential vision articulating liberation and resistance. It may be taken as an ambivalent vision of the self-locating in nativity and as an attempt to negotiate the multiple disjunctions after colonial evacuation.

The most important question is that of cultural identity, history and gender. Padhi is a poet who struggles to establish himself in the same row as discussed by several theorists and so he questions:

> Is the answer to all the endured days
> And those that wait to come,
> The uninvited answer of dreams
> Inside my intermittent sleep-
> The one that I never framed
> Nor shall ever know how I came. (13-14)

In fact, in view of semantics, post-colonialism stands for the national culture after the departure of imperial power, as a state of consciousness, a state of self-awareness, involving myth and history, language and landscape, self and the other. In the process a post-colonial poet identifies himself with contemporary India by evoking the landscape of the country, and the tradition and culture of the country. We may easily recall Eliot's "home is where one starts from" and Ezekiel's "home is where we have to gather grace".

That is why Padhi condemns the ritual of recalling the dead in his poem 'Inviting the Dead by Default',

> Everyone is busy with the ancestors–
> Their coming, going, homecoming,
> Their fulfilled wishes, strong, one-time desires
> To be restored only through the annual ritual
> Dedicated to the innumerable dead.
> ....
> ....
> The fact however is:
> I have been committing an error over
> The years and I must pay for it

Then he turns back to himself with the duallity of life and death in 'Betrayed',

This is where everything ends,
Love. The undue eagerness
To know the true picture of life.
Betrayals that death alone knows
And smiles at, the invented humility.

He is puzzled at the deeds of the past that carve out the future, and so he says in 'Small Askings',

Perhaps during all of these past days
I've only added to your waiting
for the next things to happen..(*IL*, 230, 37)

Sleepless nights torture him; he is self-conscious and this consciousness disturbs him and so he accepts in 'Attempting to Sleep Beside Oneself',

I have taken every mode of
Getting my sleep at ten.
....
....
Now sleep is awaiting my time,
Disappearing into its own kingdom
Of waiting in the adjacent room—
Its dark palace of the night. (*Titas*, 75)

He is a bit desperate, and so even in the creation of poetry he plunders the darkness of the night and finds the creation of poem as casual as child's play. In the poem 'Something Like a Poem' he says,

Yes, there's always
One more, friendless, waiting
In the dark secret premises
Of the night rain.
I know where it ism
What else it needs
In order to live in this

Rich, inhospitable world:
Waiting only to be adopted
It is raining still
And isolated poems
Are playing like children
Caring little for the darkening..... (*Reflections*, 122)

The exploration of the self is the most prominent characteristic of the post-colonial literature and particularly Indian English Poetry. Padhi's thematic range, that is better described as a 'voyage within', is the best instance of this quest; he describes the contemporary life, the individual, the family, the society. Likewise, in 'The House' he admits his attachment to his old house in a traditional way,

I've been here since the time
I learnt to know one house from another
Ther've been times when I thought
Of leaving it altogether, for ever.
Perhaps I'll never be able to do so

In 'Going to the Temple' the poet satirises the rituals performed in the mechanical way, such as washing hands, the long faces, the bountiful of offerings and a list of endless demands and so he says,

Let us wash our hands clean
Of the cruel daylight
Wipe the acquired and inherited
Meanings off our tired faces.

And in 'A World Elsewhere' he centres on his self, partly autobiographical and partly self-searching:

Not here, not here, not this, not here
....
....

No one knows, no one need know,
It is always some other lace—
The heart stealing into the might from there.

The post-colonial era has given rise to regional literature, for instance, Oriya, Bengali, Telugu, Tamil, Hindi, Kannada, etc. It is a paradoxical status to provide Indian English Literature the status of only pan-Indian literature that amalgamates all sentiments of all parts of the country as a common dais. In its treatment of themes, choice of imagery, creation of new idioms it differs from its predecessors. Padhi goes a step further when he writes some of his poems for some important men and targets something ulterior; for instance, in poem like 'Of Hiding Important Things' which is dedicated to Wiffiam Stafford, he says,

The world wouldn't take them with
A smile. I know. Or, if it did,
It'd show them up every time
You began to speak of humbler things. (11)

In 'The First Painting', dedicated to Buddhaditya, he delineates the landscape painting in a nice way,

The thick brush moves again
On the remaining space. The mark spreads
The first sun begins to shine on his face
While his eyes shine back, even though
The edges are blurred and blurring still.
My humble world begins and ends at this place. (*IS*)

And then in a mysterious way he reads a face in the dark, a poem dedicated to Siladitya, titled 'A Face in the Dark',

"Watch me, watch me carefully," it whispered,
"and you'll find the difference you never expected."(20)

While writing for Wiffliani Golding in the poem 'A Man of Our Time', he writes,

Someone somewhere would wait for you
To emerge from the haze of history
And quietly listen to what you say.
A story of our time, our place. (24)

In the poem 'Two Paintings by D. H. Lawrence' dedicated to Keith Sagar, the poet talks of 'Boccacio Story' and 'Dance Sketch', the two paintings rendering a lively picture of the landscape as a true picture,

Do trees ever combine in this
Too human way, each anxious
To touch the other in an embrace
That is unlikely to say? (40)

'Among the Ruins' is another important poem written for Shabana Azmi; in this poem we find the description of the ruins in splendid fashion,

What else is left here, except lips that
Cannot move, eyes that cannot smile?
Proud, forbidding shadows that play among
The last of the pillars, arches, family albums,
Doors and windows that never open?
No one knows; no one need know. (42)

Like a philosopher the poet visualises the world and in the poem 'The Other Place' written for Andrei Tarkovsky he wishes to glorify his presence,

Since to be here is to be everywhere,
Where was the need to go out to
A place that promised to be different?
....

> ....
> The 'other place' is here, somewhere
> Between the soul and this wintering body
> Conspiring with the soul how to prolong
> Its own impatience with time and failure. (65)

Remembering Raymond Carver in the poem 'Something Else' the poet pauses to define this something unknown,

> There's always something else to these lines,
> ....
> ....
> Always someone behind you watching.
> You know, it's always something else,
> Something other than the words in these lines. (67)

Padhi talks of the traditional town Cuttack in a very different way in his poem 'Paper Town',

> Cuttack was being re-enacted by delicate hands.
> ....
> We know more about Cuttack than you or anyone
> Of your mad friends do, my six year son proudly claimed.
> ....
> I went in; he was right, perfectly so
> His good friends were trying desperately
> To retrieve the town from a terrible mess
> That could only take care of itself. Tomorrow (34)

In 'Ceasework' the poet denounces the progress of democracy that failed to uplift the poor and remained crippled so far,

> Elsewhere, I imagine, the ministers
> Are discussing the newest ways
> Of raising public taxes, the need
> Of the currency changing hands,
> Among whispers.— The poor have remained so
> Since the time our grandfathers
> Dreamt of their homes, land, and wives. (35)

The country has become a puppet in the hands of the political leaders and the destiny of the poor is decided by them,

> Their words define
> Our needs calculatedly, against
> The heavy backdrop of industrial
> Development, welfare of the poor. (35)

Konark is the symbol of culture and civilization, and no Indian English poet can escape it and what to talk of an Oriya poet like Bibhu Padhi. "Its quiet outwardness" that holds "the weight of centuries", the "past gestures of love and renewal" and "the long awaited anguish of fulfilment" is simply the memory of "the irreverent past". The poet questions as to how one remember thingss. This is a unique sort of experience felt and expressed in a poem. Like a true post-colonial poet Padhi hints at the imperial past that has destroyed the town in the poem 'The Burnt Town',

> The town is filled with wounds
> From burns that a fire of the past
> Inflicted on it years ago
> ....
> Songs of heros could be heard
> Over he radio, the television celebrates
> The country's fortieth anniversary
> Of independence from alien hands.(45)

The poet questions,

> What have we been waiting for since then? (45)

And answers himself,

> —this waiting for
> the body's countless failures.(45)

In the poem 'Neglected Absences', he interprets things of the past and talks of the old beliefs,

> The burden of things is increasing
> Until, one day, these sinking hands
> Will fail to carry them through time.
> ....
> ....
> The old belief in everything to be where
> They are, increasing in weight
> Through common night and day. (49)

He is very meticulous in his approach and so in the poem 'The Captive Hand' he says, "Today we shall talk of the small things". In search of the lost ancestral bliss the poet talks in the poem 'Acquaintance with Fire',

> Today we wait for its childish pranks too–
> Of making a fire that we are yet to see
> Of putting together vegetables, fruits, diapers
> And written words into a utensil large enough
> To hold such other things that we feign possessing
> Giving us back what we always wanted
> The astral heat of the stars' light, the light, the light
> Of an irretrievably-lost ancestral bliss. (53)

Padhi, as if quoting from the religious scriptures, cites the do's and do-nots for man. In the poem 'Trees, Far and Near' he says,

> Each man who climbed up in the hope
> That gravity's strange tricks
> Would return him to where he came
> From, initially, has found himself fulfilled.
> ....
> That's where
> One begins to rest at the end of whims
> And failures of this life, away from the puzzle
> That might hold others in loving company. (54)

All the texts cited above vindicate Padhi's exceptional poetic qualities as a true Indian English poet, consequential to the post-colonial epoch, its urges and aspirations. He has been specified as "inward looking—deeply rooted in cultural and interpersonal realities speaking to the heart in their own universal language". That is why he is compared with great poets like A.K. Ramanujan, Kamala Das, T.S. Eliot, N.Ezekiel, R. Parthasarathy, etc.

References

Indian Literature, vol. no. 230, Nov.-Dec. 2005.

Interview with Bibhu Padhi, by Jaydeep Sarangi, in *JSL*, Spring, 2006

Padhi, B., *Painting the House*, 1999, Disha Books, Orient Longman, Mumbai.

Reflections, 2005, Vol.nos.1&2, W&W Bhagalpur.

Titas, Vol.1, Feb. 2005.

8

Wordsworth's Obsession: "Death as a State Applicable to My Own Being"

Death has been a recurrent theme of a good number of poets, and to some, almost an obsession, but the Romantics are less scared of it. In case of Wordsworth it is more conspicuous, rather a cause of fear psychosis (so to say), haunting him right from his childhood. This paper intends to trace the said elements in his poetry, the obsession of mortality with this great nature poet.

To begin with, his 'Intimations Ode' may be cited; he himself admits in a note on the poem,

> Nothing was more difficult for me in childhood than to admit the notion of death as a state applicable to my own being (because of) a sense of inimitableness of the sprit within me. I used to brood over the stories of Enoch and Elijah, and almost persuaded myself that whatever might become of others, I should be translated in something of the same way to heaven. Many times while going to school have I grasped at a wall or tree to recall myself from this abyss of idealism to the reality.

The poem begins with a sense of loss, 'a spiritual crisis', that finally leads to the thought of man's mortality. Like a child, he perceives the glorious association of the visionary gleam that is lost now: the ability to distinguish between subjects, to identify himself with the universe; he is metaphorically blind: "The fullness of your bliss, I feel—I feel it all I hear, I hear with joy I hear." The poet's sense of loss is embarrassing:

> Now, while the birds thus sing a joyous song, And while the young lambs found
> As to the tabor's sound
> To me alone there came a thought of grief

M. Bowra finds the poems as "a personal document", "the crown" of his work, that came after "the failure of his hopes in the French Revolution" and though he does not agree, he suffered from the "dissociations of power",

> Turn wheresoever I may
> By night or day
> The things which I have seen I can see no more

He has lost "celestial light", "visionary gleam" and "the glory and the freshness of a dream" and so the concluding section of the poem ends with the questions,

> Whither is fled the visionary gleam?
> Where is it now, the glory and the dream?

For him the loss of infancy, is the loss of all: "Heaven lies about us in our infancy",

> At length the man perceive it die away
> And fade into the light of common day.

Wordsworth is simply amazed at the child of his poem who can see God's glory but cannot understand it whereas the adult can no longer perceive his home in God. He can understand it through his memories of childhood, "a fleeting perception", and yet blind, and so enters into a compromise,

> We will grieve not, rather find
> Strength in what remains behind
> In the faith, that looks through death,
> In years that bring philosophic mind.

The poet does not assume a dominating didactic posture, rather he attempts to apprehend truth that is general and operative. He follows the fluxes and refluxes of the mind in a state of excitement; such an exercise involves simultaneous exercise of both feeling and thinking, with interplay of hesitation, assertion and affirmation, with the shift in his attitude, a change from the mimetic to the expressive, tending towards subjectivity, a sceptic questioning adoption of a creed distinguished by an alteration between assertion and doubt, etc. In the 'Ode' the movement between confidence and diffidence is not the structural pivot but rather a comparative assurance of the poet's beliefs and their general acceptance. In a letter to Catherine Clarkson in January 1815, he maintains,

> The poem rests entirely upon two recollections of childhood, one that of a splendour in the objects of sense which is passed away, and the other an indisposition to bend to the law of death as applying to our particular case. (1937, 619)

The poet's journey through assertions, doubts and hopes reaches a point where it is poised for the decisive release of tension and confident assertion. His pendulous movement of the mind, between assertion and doubt, values and dejection culminates in the Christian answer to despondency, and in 'The Wanderer', he sums up,

> Is Man
> A child of hope? Do generations press
> On generations, without progress made?
> Among so many shadows, are the pains

And penalties of miserable life,
Doomed to decay, and then
expire in dust!

Fear intensifies, melancholy deepens and sadness multiplies; the poet is highly aggrieved, in 'Resolution and Independence' it is discernable,

And fears and fancies thick upon me came;
Dim sadness—and blind thought, I knew not, nor could name.
and his leech—gatherer wholly exhausted—
Such seemed this Man, not all alive nor dead,
Nor all asleep- in extreme old age.

Let us come to a small poem 'A Slumber Did My Sprit Seal' (1799); its second stanza is significant in this connection,

No motion has she now, no force,
She neither hears nor sees;
Rolled round in earth's diurnal course,
With rocks, and stones and trees

This stanza is as calm as the death itself; bitter and desolate, insecure and inanimate, true and harsh mortality rolled in Nature. 'The Prelude' is another significant milestone that establishes this fact; its beginning and end is eloquent enough. The poem begins with "Dust as we are" and ends in "we are as dust"—the immortal spirit grows; this awareness of immortality grows out of the compulsions of mortality that irks the poet continually, and our ignorance towards,

The dignity of individual Man,
Of Man, no composition of the thought,
Abstraction, shadow, image, but the man
Of whom we read, the man whom we
With our own eyes...

It is too much rationalism that has kept ourselves away from our real selves and what Wordsworth calls,

> The world is too much with us

Rationalism is a self-assertive desire to categorize where an individual is simply a sum of elements that permeates, informs and finds intimately together, where individuality becomes meaningless and "substitutes a universe of death/For that which moves with light and life informed/Actual, divine and true"; it is all "where Reason seemed the most to assert her sights", and the poet reiterates,

> Not in Utopia, subterranean fields,
> Or same sacred island, Heaven knows where
> But in the very world, which is the world
> Of all of us the place where, in the end,
> We find our happiness, or not at all.

It is here that Wordsworth is called the earliest of moderns, who responded sincerely to the "Industrial Civilization with its complicated and conflicting ideologies and doubts", and "human nature with aspects of consciousness and being; still relevant to our modern interests and predicaments". His 'The Prelude' deals in existentialist philosophy, quest of identity and self-discovery, crumbling orthodoxies and dissolving certainties like true modern: "I seem! Two consciousness, conscious of myself! And of some other being". That is why, 'The Prelude' is taken to be an ancestral work for Tennyson, Eliot, Yeats, Wallace Stevens, Hopkins and Joyce. Wordsworth's London is akin to Eliot's London (that we find in his 'The Waste Land'), Baudelaire's Paris, James Joyce's Dublin and that in inferno. In politics, his anguish swings from revolutionary idealism to the tyrannical despair that is akin to prophetic paradigm of the states of mind of a lot of modern liberals. His poetry establishes the fact, that utopian ideology has been corrupted and corroded by the appetite for power. "Sick, wearied only with contraries", reveals his mental cries that is the direct consequence of lack of unity, integrity, wholeness and this compels his quest for identity, as in 'Tintern Abbey': 'And I have felt,/A presence that disturbs me with joy. And in the mind of man/A motion and a spirit, that impels/All thinking things, all object of thought/All rolls through all things". In the 'General Introduction' of Coleridge's *The Complete Works* edited by W.G T. Shedd we are convinced of the fact that we should be able to repudiate the delusions of childhood while growing into a man:

> Ingratitude, sensuality, and hardness of heart, all flow from this source. Men are ungrateful to others only when they have ceased to look back on their former selves with joy and tenderness. They exist in fragments. Annihilated as to the past, they are dead to the future, or seek for the proofs of it everywhere, only not in themselves. (1884, 46)

Wordsworth's philosophy of faith or creed stems out of his felt experience, and the divine exploration and values three things only that is God, Man and Nature. He confesses his faith in 'The Prelude', but he had to revise his opinion when he was betrayed by the ineradicable weakness of civilized man; thereafter he shifted to rationality and morality, as an orthodox Christian. His faith comprises a little of pantheism, something of Hegelian (That is, the power of human mind) and a bit dogmatic Christianity, all creating a "deathless spirit." With Christian Church he shares his "faith in life endless", in "infinity and God" and that of human immortality. However, there is a tremendous change, and he appears to be disillusioned afterwards as he utters "because the natural man is at enmity with God" and here he is a disbeliever in Christianity. Not only that Wordsworth is also supposed to be the by-product of contraries, that of "mood of calmness" and "emotional disturbance", reflective and imitative, order and disorder; that is why the climax of 'The Prelude' is also known as 'The Imagination and Taste, How Impaired and Restored'; this unparallel power is also known as "the power to see beyond the superficial confusion of phenomenon to the laws of order and of cause which governed the world". However, the imaginations here, becomes radically creative, that is purely an internal mechanism, blending the Lockean empiricist and Platonic belief, both doctrines, as possibilities, to evoke the mystery of life, vitality and organic connection, the antithetical ideas of two Greek philosophers.

The development of Wordsworth is conspicuous in his shift from nature to man and then to his fellowman (as found in 'Tintern Abbey'), public and patriotic (1807 poems), "Complex awareness of man in his human and societal relationships" (as in 'Ode to Duty', Elegiac Stanza', and 'Immortality Odes'); he dives deep in the human heart to learn its joy and fear and becomes "his own best commentator". The strong optimist of 'Lyrical Ballads' is turned to a strange pessimist acquitting the world with amazing human relationship and handicapped humanity with infirm individuals as 'The Idiot Boy', The Blind Highland Boy', etc.; the leech-gatherer, the solitary reappear, Michael, Martha and Lucy, somehow, achieve harmony with their surroundings and elemental strength. M. Bowra is of the opinion that,

> He believed that life in towns Corrupts and deadens the finer instincts of man and that they find their true selves only in the presence of natural things. (100)

In a letter to Mrs. Clarkson, Wordsworth wrote about the 'Ode'

> The poem rests entirely upon two recollections of childhood, one that of a splendour in the objects of sense which is passed

> away, and the other in an indisposition to bend to the law of death as applying to our case. (619)

Bowra is also of the view that Wordsworth's belief in natural religion began to wane soon after the completion of the 'Ode'. (102) Caryle rhetorically described him as "a cold hard, silent, practical man, a man of an immense head and great jaws like a crocodile's." (101) That's why he finds "the world is poisoned at the heart" in 'The Boarders'. He called these cities of modern civilization as the 'Cities of Destruction', and so resolves to quit the snares of material "progress". Every civilization is an encroachment on nature and the consequence is the paling cheeks and failing nerves, and foreheads haggard with the rash of modern life. His is a prophetic protest against the unhealthiness of our civilization and drab brutality of this "machine world and of the man-state". Yet he never renounced the conviction that perception of any sort is simply a state of mind and extent of feeling, and that this material world matters least.

Most of the time, Wordsworth remains passive, unable to provide life or make the living lifeless, as in the case of the leech-gatherer, "Such seemed this Man, not all alive nor dead/Nor all asleep–in his extreme old age Motionless as a cloud the old man stood". He seeks to learn the colour of death, "Why, mother, do you look so pale, And why are you so cold", because "life was happiness to him/who had no hope, nor fear"; it is the pathetic inability of the child to understand death. The simple child of 'We Are Seven' has the same implication: "what should it know of death?" Their graves are green, they may be seen. They are dead; those two are dead/their spirits are in heaven." Death does not perturb the child but the poet seems to go after it. And so in 'The Prelude' he speaks, "A soul divine which we participate.A deathless spirit", the word "deathless" is remarkable here; he falls to dissociate himself from this troubleshooter "death" and reiterates "creature divine". He embodies Christian answer to despondency. In his introduction *The Wanderer* has the answer,

> Is Man
> child of hope? Do generations press
> On generations without progress made?
> Halt the individual, even his hairs be grey
> Among so many shadows, are the pains
> And penalties of miserable life
> Doomed to decay, and then expire in dust.
>
> (Book V. 1, 465-7 8)

He deliberately admits, "At length the Man perceives it die away/ And fade into the light of common day"; it is not the fading of childhood, rather manhood or lifehood (so to say), though he is a bit optimistic by the end of 'Ode': "We will grieve not rather find! Strength in what remains behind in the faith, that looks through death."

References

Bowra, M.C., 1999, *The Romantic Imagination*, O.U.P., New Delhi.

Hutchinson, T & Selincount, E., (ed.), 1973, *Wordsworth: Poetical Works*, O.U.P., London,

Setincount, E., (ed.), 1937, *The Letters of William and Dorothy Wordsworth: The Middle Years*, Oxford: Clarendon Press.

Shedd, W.G.T., ed., 1884, *S.T. Coleridge: The Complete Works*, New York.

9

Jayanta Mahapatra's Poetics of Confessions

To write anything about Jayanta Mahapatra may appear absurd, as he is a big name. A number of books by reputed scholars are available, yet I would like to trace his poetic contours that determine his self-imposed frontiers, and find him a muddled poet, as he himself admits, "I'm so muddled up now with English and Oriya. I'm neither here nor there.... We change with the times; we change with the years. It's difficult for me to say now what made me write them." (Panja, 26)

It is not the question of language only that he goes for; rather it is visible in his options and his anxieties: "I was in two minds when I wrote it. I would like to leave it that way." (30) "I admit there are tensions. Part of me wants to merge into the ancient Hindu culture while another part.... It is their tensions that urge me to write poetry. I can't do anything else." (32-33)

His is a life that is torn and wretched and that appears in his poetry as he tells us, "Poetry, like life, is reminiscence. I cannot separate life from poetry" (32) and "I'm shaped by factors beyond my control..... I'm not deliberately holding on to tensions.... There is a charm inside which can never be bridged." (31) "Physics taught me that all observation is uncertain, ambiguous. The ambivalent nature of intrinsic nature haunts me." (31)

From a close survey of his works *Close the Sky, Ten by Ten* (1971), *Svayamvara and Other Poems* (1971), *A Father's Hours*

(1976), *A Rain of Rites* (1976), *Waiting* (1979), *The False Start* (1980), *Relationship* (1980), *Life Signs* (1983), *Dispossessed Nests* (1986), *Selected Poems* (1987), *Burdens of Waves and Fruits* (1988), *Temple* (1989), *A Whiteness of Bone* (1992), we find his real self that defines himself. There is something in his heart that irks him and he says, "Poetry makes me write poems with a bad heart. I don't know what that exactly means, but it is the heart that makes one furry secretly into someone... pushing to choose values, attitudes and to do the not-so-obvious: this heart, as it keeps on trying to hide the wounded walls of its house, and at the same time asking itself for a meaning to our lives." (Panja, 15)

Mahapatra's making is different, and consequently the upbringing of his poetry is altogether different. This difference may be gauged as both his specialty and his frontiers. It is his options and preferences, concept and understanding, observations and record, suffering and realization, outcry and response, grabbing and manifestation that matter the most. Most of us fail to categorize him, "Unlike Ezekiel and Ramanujan, Mahapatra is difficult to read, for obscurity, complexity and allusiveness are his poetry. He is rather in the company of Shiv K.Kumar and K.N. Daruwalla... to acclimatize an indigenous tradition to English language and create a new Indian English." (Das 1)

Niranjan Mohanty is of the view, "Mahapatra discovers in culture another metaphor for identity. Mahapatra consciously and conscientiously perpetuates his journey within and towards the deposits of culture sedimented in the self." (58)

My contention moves contrary to those established by John Barnie who confirms Mahapatra "not a nihilist like Philip Larkin, where in the end, nothing is of value," compares him with Wordsworth in working "the still sad music of humanity" so movingly, and at another existence to present, "a powerful, haunting image of the world made and remade through the visionary existent." (*Journal of Commonwealth Literature*, Vol. XVIII, No. 1, 1983)

Let us take, for instance, *A Rain of Rites* (1976) and the first word is "sometimes" followed by "malignant purpose", "numbly", "quivers", "stale', concluding with "hard to overcome." His observation is inconclusive and frequently pauses at 'who,' 'whom,' 'where,' 'which' and 'what.' The poet is assailed by doubt, anxiety and inquisitive sensibility and all remains unanswered till the end of the poem and fails "before it reaches its objective." His mission of life is forfeited and "thrown like kelp on the beach/ like some shape of conscience I cannot look at/a malignant purpose in a nun's eye" (7): thereafter he proceeds to questions:

> Who was the last man on earth, to whom the cold cloud
> brought? the blood to his face?
> Numbly I climb the mountain
> top of airs
> Where my own soul quivers on the
> edge of answers (Mahapatra, 1987, 7)

And then,

> Which still, stale air sits on an angel's wings?
> What holds my rain so it's hard to overcome? (7)

The poet's problems remains unsolved: he doesn't find any answers. He believes in some negative force which holds back the rain and this disbelief amounts to his further misgivings., which others call a realistic approach and I call a half-hearted endeavour. Coming to 'A Summer Poem', we again find negative impulse: the chanting of priests "louder than ever", "the movement of crocodiles", "smoke under fire" and the good wife "unexhausted by the deep roar of funeral pyres". The imaginary of "funeral pyre" particularly is striking as it stands alone signifying nothing and Mahapatra deliberately drags the summer heat to crematorium: the common reader fails to decipher the connotation. The words "sombre", "louder", "middens", "smoke", 'long", "still" and "deep" ascertain his ambivalence, trauma and psychoses. As Mahapatra himself explains in *Contemporary Author Autobiography Series*,

> I found myself once again at the border between two separate regions of mind-between what perhaps. I understood and what I did not... which makes up my life, those blurs of vague light that pulsate with the days.... Today, the same questions bother me although I see no specific cause or rationale for such things. But such searching moves me and I am unable to resist it in my poetry. For poetry is voice "vaak" and it is a voice forged from those elements which constitute the world both within and without: a voice which carries with it its unused power of survival. (148)

Mahapatra takes his poetry as "the creation of a mind in despair" (Panja 74), "suffering with triumph and disaster", "my romance with my own land and with my innermost self."(*Contemporary Author*, 147) In 'The Lines of My Poems' Mahapatra writes,

> Today a line of this poem
> Has lost the use of its healthy legs.
> Trapped like a sparrow
> Which has strayed inside?
> Beating its wing against the
> bars of world's conscience.
> It slumps pitifully
> On the floor of the present.

Mahapatra places his poetry at the juncture of post-colonialism, in focusing the non-West or its cultural other, somehow interdisciplinary, incorporating the antagonistic theories of Darwin, Freud and Marx, which refused to be contained within the binaries of 'us' and them' and the insistence on questioning stereotypes like the oppressor/oppressed. It may be the reflection of inadequacies of anti-colonial and socio-historical pressures created by an awareness about the new imperialistic strategies operating in the political, economic and cultural sites, discernible as a process of interrogating social obligations as anti-colonial resistance. Consequently poetry is seen as seminal or instrumental exercise, shifting from Commonwealth to post-colonialism. It is a literary exercise to erase the inferiority instilled in the native minds of values caused by the psychological damage to colonized people, an aesthetic device where the writers' connections with their Third World homes become metaphorical, a sort of cultural metamorphosis. This is evident in transplantation of names, collation of language and the diversification of tastes, amplified by a coming to the polyglot metropolis. Interestingly uncompromising textual or cultural inversion has its root in old binaries of colonial ideology influencing cultural vocabulary, plagued by neo-colonial maladies like economic disorder, social malaise, state repression, power hierarchies all pointing to strategic move, securing positive reception towards creativity or urge to poetry.

Mahapatra's poetry is the kind of literature as stated by Rushdie in *Imaginary Homelands*:

> Literature is interim report from the consciousness of the artist, and so it can never be finished or perfect. Nothing so inexact so easily and frequently misconceived deserves the protections of being declared sacrosanct.... The only privilege literature deserves... is the privilege of being the arena of where the struggle of languages can be acted out. (427)

Like Arun Kolatkar, Mahapatra is a bilingual poet and has "taste for the bizarre perspective and oblique entry point into situations wry irony underpins the miracle of things seen and touched, people met and sized up the epic alternates with the intimates, the self weaves through the other... tempted into cynicism but mandated to bear witness to history... addressed mythic themes that still resonate in India's public life." (The Hindu. Sept. 27, 2004)

Interestingly, he eludes to the vigilant squads of linguistic absolutism to a great extent as demotic rather than classical in his emphasis, sculpted with the chisels of awe and understanding of a commune. Yet negation follows, interrogation follows, and the poet seems helpless "looks at the girl he had once married", "the moon showering 'ghost light' that floats upon the consciousness"; he maintains his curiosity:

> Is it the earth that catches its breath?
> Or is one there?
> Only a shredded prayer... flag keeps twisting in the wind. (9)

We cannot make out why Mahapatra thinks of the unfulfilled, unattended and unfathomed side of the world: all his queries lead to abstainism. He is aware of his limitations and he accepts it in his own essay 'The Absence of Absolutes,'

> An ingrained sadness never left me.... It seemed natural to me that I would shy away from the ostentatious community of human relationship.... I began to write in the manner I experienced living; feeling the wrong, the lie, the nastiness and the injustice I perceived around me: and could go on to question the existence of God whom my parents had taught me scrupulously to believe in... only there was a strange agency in me I couldn't put aside... slowly there emerged from my life an intriguing, melancholy poetry... discontent helped me to write... in a way we are all participating in the catastrophes of the would.

Obviously, Mahapatra is a fragmented soul—sad, elusive, amazed—and all these find place in his poetry. His search of his own self in Somewhere My Man' discloses the secret in a better way. He searches himself by the riverbank seclusions, in his daily routine, in the happenings of the world and finally concludes with "Nothing matters'. He finds his man,

> Here sits my man
> in the doorway of a dunged street.
> beside his ailing mother her pinched aged face
> proudly bearing
> the irrelevance of movement. (11)

He raises questions but cannot answe. For him "A man does not mean anything" because he presumes place more significant, a man becomes the place and "Here is the hour that will not move" and then "What use is there, tearing a country to bits?" and finally "nothing matters". This journey of man from riverbank to daily life and subsequently to the concern of country signifies Shakespeare's design "sound and fury signifying nothing." We fail to understand the poet's intention: does he think me is static?: does he calculate man always as "ailing", "irrelevance" and likewise? Why he prefers to nullify man? Why he has made a man non-entity? He is deep in pain and his suffering is endless that is why 'Dhauli' concludes,

> The measure of Asoka's suffering
> does not appear enough.
> The place of his pain peers lamentably
> from among the pains of the dead. (22)

All of a sudden, we are compelled to infer thats the preordained place of the individual within this world is to be found in the trivial terms of a modern Western quest for identity and the poet transplants this into his contemporary Indian social milieu. However the stubborn nomadic existence of the individual resists dreams and alternatives and ends up doing whatever it has been ordained to. This is the most distinct trend of Indian English poetry which started with 'mimicry,' adopted 'hybridity' and finally culminated in 'identity' (quest); this is the structure of our own epistemological make-up as of dialectically creative historical process.

Rain of Rites (1976), *Waiting* (1979), *The False Start* (1980), *Relationship* (1980), *Life Signs* (1983) and *Burden of Waves and Fruit* (1986) constitute the gist of Mahapatra's poetry. He rushes to 'the rain' for most of his expressions and creativity. The rain refreshes him; it stirs his inside, it purgates him, helps him in his confessions and 'nothing matters' as he proceeds towards nothingness with rain for sheer fulfilment. From 'Summer,' to 'My Man,' 'Puri' to 'Mythology,' from 'Sunburst' to 'Hunger,' from 'Faith' to 'Future,' from 'Indian Way' to 'Country Festival' he feels 'Pain' of the 'Dark' 'Ash' and 'Moon.' The taboos of the Indian Way ("I could not touch you, like that"), the anxiety of the future ("The world's the same/ It's the future's face he would not offend"), the superstition of a country festival ("a priest's butting nose.... Like wild water snakes/left loose from the yearly floods"), the interrogations of the pain ("when will my eye return/ that has been swallowed by the sky/what ceremony veils its world?"), the unknown world of the dark ("Just the sound of something vague/slipping away from the old mind's grasp/of something hatching alone on the unknown leaf"), the aftermath of a rainy day ("who knows/what's dying underneath/a growing blade of grass/Or what habit palpitates"), the futile rigidity of the mountain ("it gives clear proof that one might reconstruct one's life. Rigid/yet strongly impotent"), the substance of the ash ("the dumb order of the myth bodiless grains") question of the moon moment ("How can I stop the life 1 lead within myself?") and the disturbing "Godly and Great" ("what use is history if it gives sanction to creation of things?")—all goes in the creation of *Waiting* and *The False Start.* Most probably *Waiting* intends to wait for a better future of our culture and civilization and *The False Start* wanders in the mysterious hazards of nature. In *Relationship*, he analyzes himself in relationship with the vicinity:

> We have come as dreams
> disguised that pinned us down.
> ... ...
> ... ...
> Only that the stones were my very own
> Waiting as mother or goddess or witch
> as my birth feeds on them
> as though on the empty dugs of
> sorcerous thought
> ... ...
> ... ...
> Where cranes found into the surrounding silence
> and the clouds shift with the tears
> of wounded pools of our living ... . going nowhere
> ... ...
> ... ...
> It is my own life
> That has concerned me beneath the stones
> of the temple in ruins, in a blaze of sun. (38-46)

And concludes:

> This must be the myth of every happiness...
> where only ideas, like brooms,
> wait oddly on their unstable heads (47)

In *Life Sign*, his endeavour is to extract meaning out of our movements, our actions and our reactions; "So we drag meanings/ from what we see"; he express his inability most often: "I am unable to force an answer out of you/wherever I try to live" and "It is not simple to share love/with those who live in us" and "In this time of darkness the lost ones and I/will dim like lamps and go back to the movements/we caught once in the uncertain light of dawns." (64) He struggles to find, "My silence here gives off no light/a slow mist still fights the eyes/for life's present symmetry" (65) and "Thanking, to escape his beliefs/I go to meet the specter of belief" (66) and then he calls, "There is a dawn waiting beside us, whose signs/are a hundred-odd years away from you." (68) He is awestruck at his own ignorance: "I wonder where the day goes/even in the bright seen/this was a world I did not know" (69) and "I try to make myself more than what I am." (70) He merges with nature "Haunted by birds of prey where strange trees grow/deep in the hills of my blood, that river flows", (71) In a summer afternoon his mind visits hospital and finds pain, "And time drawn like a thin wind/to the shape of pain"(72) and he confesses "I answer from no clear place I am in." (73) The twilight appears to be curse, "Its cry/a plea to share in its curse" (74) and the event that attracts is, "A rape penetrates the periphery of the jungle/And thought looks up/dumbly at the toes of words." (75) Mahapatra questions himself, "Do we have to be uncertain of ourselves" (76) and the reason he finds, "Because every one believes that it moves with us/ and yet no one believes it until we find ourselves." (78)

We are surprised to find such a great poet leaning towards nothingness, but he admits:

> As a poet, I think I am both an observer and a participant in life. Many apparently unnoticed events too, make fleeting contacts with the mind, and the impression left behind provided substance and device for what I want to write.... My purpose in writing has to share with the reader the hearts, soul and daily lives of my people including, myself. (113)

So is Mahapatra, confined in his own world of observation, that of Orissa and his "rain" fails to devour his "darkness, nothingness and death" and he remains,

like a lone rain,
no more eager for answers
Just pure flies
keeps on breathing from
Our open eyes. ('Dance of the Fire Flies')

And Mahapatra's ritual of exploring his own self is yet incomplete, as he admits in an interview to S.K. Banerjee, "Maybe my poems are a ritual towards finding myself finding the other one inside me ambiguities still remain.... No, I don't think I have still found 'the other one' inside me" (*Journal of Literature and Aesthetics*, 85)

Mahapatra answers his own yearnings in his essay 'The Voice in the Ink': "My poetry suffers from such endless questioning, and also from the cliched subjects of time, death, and the quest which man is after." (12) He is "an ignorant man, almost a poet" as confessed by a great philosopher, Santayana.

References

Das, B.K., 2001, *The Poetry of Jayanta Mahapatra*, Atlantic.

Mahapatra, J., *Contemporary Author, Autobiography Series*, Michigan, Vol.1, Detroit: Gale.

______ 1987, *Selected Poems,* O.U. P.

______ 2002, "My Poetry: A Small, Late Wish", *Journal of Literature and Aesthetics*, Vol. 2, No.1, Jan.-June, p.113.

______ 2003, "The Absence of Absolutes", *Haritham*, Vol.15.

______ 2001, "The Voice in the Ink", *Haritham*, Vol.13.

Mohanty, N., "Language, Culture and Identity: A Study in the Poetry of Nissim Ezekiel and Jayanta Mahapatra", *Reflections*, Vol.1, No.1& 2.

Panja, S., (ed.), 2001, *Many Indians, Many Literatures: New Critical Essays,* Worldview, Delhi.

Rushdie, S., 1991,*Imaginary Homelands,* New York: Granta Books, in association with Viking.

10

Meena Alexander in Her Exile

The word 'exile' is very much torturing and suffocating to one and all and particularly to Meena Alexander whose migration is voluntary but not to her contentment evident in her works, such as *Fault Lines: A Memoir* (1993), *The Sock of Arrival: Reflections on Post-Colonial Experience* (1997), *Manhattan Music* (1997), and the poetry collections *The Bird's Bright Ring* (1974), *I Root My Name* (1977), *Without Place* (1978) *Stone Roots* (1980), *House of a Thousand Doors* (1985), *River and Bridge* (1995). She explains her stand and understanding clear in the 'Preface' of *Without Place*,

> English in India is a nowhere language-spatially, it does not belong anywhere and so its poet, as one who would make this very habitation in the language of his most vital speech necessary groups himself as exiled. And those who have not raised or sunk their voice to consciousness of exile everywhere bespeak it by virtue of the tongue they use. (viii)

She also tries to define the term 'exile' as "one who is estranged from place around him, his body cannot appropriate its given landscape."(viii) M. K. Naik elaborates her poetic personality as below,

> Meena Alexander is a poet with a wide range of reference her roots are firmly planted in her native Kerala soil. Hence, while

> reacting to her Western experience, her mind keeps on making an effortless transition to the eastern milieue.(193-94)

Satish Kumar is of the view,

> Melancholy, death, devaluation of values in life character her poetry. Warmth of feeling and the intensity of passion are conspicuous in her poetry. (316)

In *The Bird's Bright Ring* we have the evidence of Kumar's assertion where she pens,

> Breath of my breath
> Be to me
> As a far stat flashing
> And in this dark flesh
> Trace your lean rare watching
> So keep pace with my bare pulse
> Which times is fast out racing.

Apart from her concern for the exile, she is deeply entrenched in the political development not only of her parent country, that is, India, but of the whole world, and thus the themes of her poems vary from South Africa's Nelson Mandela to the Babri Masjid demolition. For Ayodhaya episode she writes,

> Hundreds hacked to death in Ayodhya in Ram's golden name.

She prefers to talk through symbols and so her images are more accurate and pertinent to portray the witnessed scenario and produce the desired effect; thus Unit-XI of the book *The Bird's Ring* tells us something more than the surface meaning of the used words,

> the shadow of the British soldiers and they dragged their guns over the slope to the cleft of the Ridge 1857 a cold bad winter and they broke our backs. (19)

The use of the specific years of 1857 is a deliberate application of the particular time-frame to manifest the excuse of the colonial age which extends even after Independence and manifested in the period of Emergency clamped on India territory by Indira Gandhi and its disastrous repercussions. As her memory trades back, she unravels the complex of the past to make it noteworthy in the present,

> Not only shadows fell that cold hand winter
> But bruises like down from hidden veins of porphyry
> As the belly of the mother
> Was torn open. (20)

The colour 'red' is the colour of blood and brutality used time and again symbolizing inhumanity, tyranny and coldness of the British rule and the autocratic design of functioning of political mafia today. Her concern is the enmeshed entities of the countries of the world and the most frequently in news, that of India and Pakistan, which she talks of,

> Cobber
> Howker
> Beggar man
> Thief
> Who were butchered
> In the fight between
> two fierce Kingdoms.

The kingdoms mentioned here are that of these twins. Like a sensible intellectual she dislikes the phenomenal blunder of partition and calls it "Fragil as the filament of an egg", and "glittering obsidian". She terms it, "your birth/an endless devastation/the devastation of morality." Stream of consciousness and dramatic monologue are the two techniques which have been employed to express warmth of feeling and intersity of passion though immaculate and flawless language, picturesque images, and brilliant technical excellence. Bruce King is of the viev' that,

> Meena Alexander, in contrast to Eunice de Souza, is inclined towards poetry that is incantatory and meditational. Memories, desires and fiction merge as she examines the construction of her identity and its relationship to family history, actuality, being a woman and writing poetry. (310)

She has written individual poems and her creative capability appears to be "a world of process" rather than fixity. Her deep concern is that of woman and her native land, hence she dwells on "phenomenology and woman in Romanticism", the feminine self and the life in diaspora. Perhaps, she is more conscious of her, identity as poets as John Keats feels,

> A poet is most impractical of anything in existence, because he has no iden,tity, he is continually informing and filling same other body. The sun, the moon, the sea and men and women who are creature of impulse are poetical and have about them an unchangeable attribute, the poet has none; no identity. (letter to Richard Woderhouse, Oct.27,1 818)

In the twenty-first century, there is tremendous pressure of organised crime, violence, sabotage, disintegration and disguised exploitation which have marginalized the identity of man as a being and hence it has become imperative for all of us to take a firm stand and assert our identity to save the dignity of man. Meena Alexander is also in search of her identity and in the process identifies herself with the proletariate and says,

> I sing for all work head bent
> Close against the great re sun
> Who labour tooth nail sinew bone
> Against glass metal paper store. (15)

Here she is close to the Marxian approach by voicing the 'have nots'. She also has an erroneous impression of the urban woman and so resolves to reprimand her,

> Woman of Delhi!
> You do not see how centuries of dreams
> Are flowing from your and. (15)

Her diasporic entity is nostalgic at times, recalling her mother, her unfulfilled desire and her early days. It is terribly acute and dominant in her poetry of the post-expatriation period. She also indulges in writing reflective poetry about which M. K. Naik says,

> Alexander's reflective poems are far less successful. Lacking a solid ground in external reality, they tend to be obscured by half articulated thought in dangerous league with private significance, resulting in a miasma of vaguely conveyed meaning. (194)

Interestingly, Meena Alexander is more ironical and wittier than her predecessors, yet her anguish is conspicuous: of her immigrant self and her multicultural background. Any woman can find her expanding horizons in Alexander's poems as a woman has created herself today or has become out of circumstances. She is a post-colonial phenomenon and the colonial sensibility is very much irritating to her. It was so pinching that she opted to change her name as she admits in her autobiography *Fault Lines*,

> I felt I had changed my name
> To what I already was some
> Truer self, stripped free of
> The colonial burden. (74)

The word 'Meena' means 'fish' in Sanskrit, 'jewelling' in Urdu, and 'port' in Arabic; her choice reflects her multi-lingual nature.

The wound of migration persists throughout her life and she mentions it is her autobiography,

> I am, a woman cracked my multiple migrations. Uprooted so many times she can connect nothing with nothing. (3) ....I am a poet writing in America. But American poet?... An Asian American poet then?... Poet tout count?... A woman poet, a woman poet of colour, a South Indian woman who makes up lines in English.... A Third World woman poet...? (193)

Such questions highlight the issues of multiculturalism and hybridity available in the Indian English poetry of the diasporic section'. She is also a post-colonial self and so goes for the themes of national as well as personal significance, and struggles to establish her identity with dignity. So her poems lapse into autobiographical sketches. As a diasporic entity she has to face the problem of race and nationality; she describes it in the poem 'Night Science, the Garden',

> My back against barbed wire
> Snagged and coiled to belly height
> On granite post
> Glittering to the moon
> ....
> ....
> No man's land
> No woman's either
> I stand in the middle of my life.

Here, Meena Alexander uses strong and powerful imagery to convey her ideas and attitudes. In *House of a Thousand Doors* (1988) she creates her emotional world of images, symbols and obsessions: houses representing maternal family (Kerala), a feminist consciousness and nostalgic yearnings, and the tool used for the purpose is the memories.

The Storm: A Poem in Five Parts (1989) introduces fans made by folding a sheet of paper and reading a poem like watching the scenes on such a fan, a sort of feminine world. In *Night-Scene, the Garden* (1992), again, we have the image of her maternal home and her woman companion of childhood; she finds the role of a poet most adequate to possess the world. She creates her own self though writing, with the help of abstract symbols like, the sky, the stars, the sun accompanied by mental focus, "obsessions, desires and essential loneliness." She has been influence by phenamenological approach to the existence of the self and its expression in art. *The Sock of Arrival: Reflections on Post-Colonial Experience* (1997) has both her autobiographical prose and verse which is a post-colonial trait of a discourse mingling different titerary genres, even autobiography to show her multicultural stance/make-up. Her inner core is always in search of self-articulation and definition in the ever-changing world-scenario. In the poem 'Golden Horizon', she rates herself,

> I
> ....
> "so what's it like there?", She asked.
> I replied: "As the Hudson pours
> The river wall clings tight with glinting stones.
> Yet what's so bright makes for odd imaginings
> Sometimes feel as if a metal bowl had split
> Dented by blows from a woman's fist
> And bits of spelling lessons shards of script
> Stuck from a past locked into privacy
> This is the immigrant's fury no?
> Who understand my speech,
> Further what is my speech?
> Dropped, pounding as rice grains might".

In her nostalgic move, she creates not only her past, but also the characters that mattered in her making. In 'Her Garden' or "Looking Rough Well Water' she recalls her grandmothers,

I'll tell you what divides us:
a ridge of cloud, two oceans,
a winter in my fireless room
high above Van Cortlandt Park
also death, the darkest water
crashing through pebbles, fern
fronds, bits of speckled shell.

In the process of search, she discovers herself in different forms, identified with different objects, individuals and situations,

Who can cry back into a first world
A barefoot child on a mud forking paths,
Fields gold with monsoon water,
Haunt of the snail and dragonfly?
What makes the narrative whole?
Beneath my check I feel her belly's bowl
Thick with blood, the woman who waits for me.
Are these her lips or mine?
Whose tongue is this
Melting to the quick of migrancy?

Surprising, the use of English language as conveyance of emotions and ideas also inks her a lot, because she finds it as a betrayal of her nationality and the past laden with rich tradition and is nothing but "no man's land." She regards English as leftover of colonialism and locates the imprint of the British in so Independence culture, as she writes,

> Colonialism seems intrinsic to the burden of English in India, and I felt robbed of literacy in my own mother tongue.... There is a violence in the very language. American English, that we have faced, even as we work to make it ours, decolonize it so that it will express the truth of bodies beaten and banned. After all, for such as we are, the territories are not free. (82)

So repelling is the alien flavour and its ingredient yet the multicultural status drives her to espouse it making it irresistible.

A similar sentiment can be traced in other diasporic writers, in their prodigious mode to identify themselves with their culture and location, at all levels, national, transnational and personal.Though placed in different environments and move with different attitudes and expressions; it is a move "to resist and to belong" with different dynamics of desire. It is a reflection of her plurality and hybridity, a creation out of cultural plantation, a fragment of her inheritance, and at times, a stranger to herself.

11

Indian English Poetry: Nissim Ezekiel's India

> A man can do something for and in his environment by being full what he is, by not withdrawing from it. I have not withdrawn from India.

This is what Ezekiel opines while comparing his India with the India that V. S. Naipaul has presented in his trilogy *The Wounded Civilization*, *Area of Darkness* and *Million Mutinies*. He identifies himself with India but avoids its two extremes: the sophistication of rootless and the parochialism of the native, to cite his own phrases. Eliot, Yeats and Auden are his three great influences from whom he could imbibe the significance of the very existence of humanity, and the world the erosion of values of all kinds, the interrogation on the identity of human beings and humanistic concern as a central creative impulse.

With a strong Jewish background, Ezekiel approaches India through its past to improve the present and correct the future. Let us start with his poem 'Patriot' which presents a fine caricature of the Indian politician:

> I am standing for peace and nonviolence
> Why world is fighting
> Why all people of the world
> Ana not following Mahatma Gandhi
> I am simply not understanding. (*CP*, 237)

Ezekiel in a satirical vein/tone presents before us the true picture of our political leaders whose patriotism is nothing but hypocrisy to win the innocent hearts of poor and illiterate Indians. They have no idea of the heterogeneous social and cultural system of this subcontinent and the idea of world peace or Ram-Rajya is a day-dream for them. In his poem 'Poverty', he attempts to expose the bitter truth of hunger and nakedness. In the poem titled 'The Professor', the real status of a retired teacher—Professor Seth—whose bankruptcy of ideas and attitude makes him pathetic. He does not possess any plan of progress, rather he is proud of his eleven children:

> These are days of family planning I am not against. We have to change with times whole world changing, In India also we are keeping up. Our progress is progressing. Old values are going, new values are coming.(*CP*, 239)

His sense of complacency and belongingness is vague and a big nonsense,

> If you are coming again this side by chance visit please my humble residence also I am living just an opposite house's backside.(*CP*, 239)

We have a series of poems where we can very easily diagnose his critical stance of the Indian population, for example, the poems, 'Songs for Nandu Bhendi', 'Under trial Prisoner', 'Song to be Shouted Out', 'Family', 'Night of the Scorpion', 'Nude 1978', etc. In the poem 'Songs for Nandu Bhindi', we are acquainted with feelings and emotions of common man and in the poem 'Under Trial Prisoners', we get acquainted with the ambiguous status of law and order and the miserable status of prisoners,

> Thousands like him
> Who did something wrong

Five years ago or may be ten
They don't know when
They were offered bail
But did not have money
So they live in jail. (*CP*, 241)

Decolonization brought modernity for which India was not ready at all; yet the affluent class grabbed it impatiently and urban mass was most afflicted, be it individual, family or society. In 'Song to be Shouted Out', we have such a family, where the wife hurls a humble of questions to her husband,

Did you post that letter?
Did you make that telephone call?
Did you pay that bill?
What do you do all day? (*CF*, 242)

The husband is helpless and finds himself to be destined to be so,

It's good for my soul
To be shouted at
Shout at the women!
What else are wives for? (*CF*, 242)

This is the plight of a helpless urbanized husband, who has to face a volley of queries, harsh treatment, and all adjustment. This is how India has changed, a shift from established norms to initiated designs. On the other hand, the country is peopled by hypocrite religious gurus preaching 'isms' of different sorts and dividing the country in various sects and sections,

Let father go to Rajneesh Ashram
Let mother go to Gita classes
What we need is meditation
Need to find our root, Sir,
All of us are sick, Sir, (*CP*, 243)

The poem 'Family' dramatizes the pseudo-sickness of a family which is not a physical one rather psychological or intellectual, a result of institutionalized falsehood, a modern mask of sophistication and variety. Like A.K. Ramanujan, Ezekiel too is conscious of his roots and attacks the rootlessness of modern man.

"I stand only by poetry", that is what he says and applies to his practical life and so in London he had only three companions, "philosophy, poverty and poetry". With the Sahitya Akademi Award 1983, he emerged as the most prominent poet of the post-independence era. We can easily diagnose a remarkable correlation between his poetic theory and poetry, because he had a refined critical sensibility and his poetic crude is based on his practical experience of the art of creativity.

His specialty is his Indianness to which he adheres in all its vicissitudes: its society, religion, love, sex, culture, family, hypocrisy, corruption, ideology and frustration. Thus, in the poem entitled 'The Double Horror', it is the corruption that intrigues the poet and he admits,

> I am corrupted by the world, continually
> Reduced to something less than human by the crowd
> Newspaper, cinemas, radio features, speeches
> Demanding peace by man with grim war like faces,
> Posters selling health and happiness in bottles,
> Large returns for small investment

Ezekiel finds himself corrupted within and without; it is the sick environment which has spoiled everything including the psyche of the poet and now he fears,

> Corrupted by the world I must infect the world
> With my corruption. This double horror holds me
> Like a nightmare from which I cannot wake, enounced
> Only by myself, to others harmless, here,

Sage, poet, conversationalist, connoisseur
Of coffee, guide to modern Indian art
Or greek antiquities. Only being what I am
Hunts, and hunts the world and me there is a frightful
Equipoise, as infected I corrupt the world.

'Entertainment' is a satirical poem with ironical presentation of the morality of a civilized society through the monkey-show,

The monkey-show is on;
Patient girl on haunches
Holds the strings.....
Only the monkeys are sad....
Anticipating times for payment
The crowed dissolves .....
The show moves on,

Here we have a combination of realism and irony exposing the absurdity of the affluent class of society, caring least for the poor. It also revels the poet's concern for the animals that are tortured and used by men to earn money or otherwise. The poet visits the downtrodden seeking social justifice in the name of division of labour.

He talks of the differences between the rich and the poor defined by their earning and created by disparity in wages and salary, for the simple reason that the demands of everyone of us persists as it is determined by our aspirations, which is identical for all of us. The result is the hue and cry to get more and more money from any source, and here comes corruption and all immoral gestures to settle complications. The poet chooses 'The Railway Clerk' to expose this malaise,

Money, money, where to get money?
My job is such, no one is giving bribe
While other clerks are in fortunate position,
And no promotion even because I am no graduate.

Here we can recall the story 'The Necklace' which displays the same traumatic experience. To the poor-paid employee morality is meaningless; things like scruples and conscience are of no use, and they wish to have more and more money to meet the day-to-day compulsions of life. It is the real status of the poor and helpless Indians. Similar is the fate of a flood victim 'Yaswant Jagtap',

> He is sixty, the child eleven,
> He pushes a handcart
> Earns a rupee a day.
> A true-blue Indian he
> Is reconciled to his lot
> And so are we.

In the poem entitled 'Healers', Ezekiel talks of sorts of saints with their mysterious way of healing:

> God's love remains your heritage
> You need not change
> Your way of life
> Know your mantra, mediate,
> Release your kundalini
> Get your shakti awakening
> And float with the spirit
> To your destinations

Ezekiel does not stroll back to the past for the theme of his poetry. He creates out of 'slum and skyscraprers' and his growth of mind is by inhospitable city-life. B.K Das opines,

> If Wordsworth could measure his life with 'mountains and valleys, and Eliot with 'Coffee spoon', then Ezekiel does so with 'slums and skyscrapers'. Therein comes his resolution: 'I cannot leave this island/I was born here and belong. (33)

Like Dom Moraes, R. Parthasarathy and A.K. Ramanujan he does not face the problem of belonging on homelessness or alienation, rather his fastidious and firm-rooted conviction which guide him through his entire poetic career. Definitely, this is a positive quality which involves and strengthens the concept of nationality, identity, culture and indianness in all its colour and texture.

Ezeekiel's 'Latter-Day Psalms' incorporates India in all its essence, B.K. Das is of the view:

> The author as a person may be absent from his work, but he is present in it 'as a certain functional' principal 'which limits, excludes and chooses in order to bring an organic relationship between the various texts of the author…as a man strives to exist in a modern urban society, to search for truth and to realize identity with the self and the community, his struggles, failures an frustrations revels not only his own inward nature but also the insufficiency and frailty of the fallen city.... (33-34)

In *Letter-Day Psalms* we have like 'Healers', 'Hangovers' 'Jewish Wedding in Bombay', 'Very Indian Poems in India English', 'Undertrial Prisoners', 'Song to be Shouted Out', 'Touching', 'Family', etc., reflect Indianness: their poverty, superstition, hypocrisy in the name of religion.

> The unplanned city has a death-wish everybody is in the business, buying curves so the healers came in droves.

Not only is the common prevalent belief, but also the prevalent democratic system that is the target of the poet and he says in 'Undertrial Prisoners',

> We have our rule
> Made long ago
> He's got to wait
> The law says so
> It's not our fault
> He lives in jail
> He did something wrong
> And he can't pay bail...
> And he can't pay bail...

Obviously, it is not the law that has failed us but we have failed it. We are blind to the spirit of law, and as a result, crime and criminals are interpreted in a disproportionate way, judgment is delayed and innocent are kept undertrials for unnecessary long period. The poet observes the Marxist in 'Hangover':

> The expensive menu and the shadow of Marx, The Biryani
> Hyderabadi and the sighs for Bangladesh.

This is the real preference of the present day Marxist who enjoy the luxury of five-star hotels and talk about the suppressed. There is a horrible difference in their words and deeds. This is the hypocrisy of the so-called intellectuals of the day. And the Indian superstition, in the poem 'The Visitor',

> Three times the crow has cawed
> At the window
> Three times I got the message.

According to one of the superstitions if a crow caws three times a gust is likely to come into the house. The poet highlights this funny belief.

"Enterprise" is a good instance of the poet's skill to visualize India through an extended metaphor of pilgrimage covering the entire length of culture and civilization, right from its past down to the present times. It has a symbolic significance. Beginning with the Great Vedantic era, it delineates the British rule, the father of the nations, the difference between Hindus and Muslims, the Partition, the two attacks of China and Pakistan of 1962 and 1965 respectively, the creation of Bangladesh in 1971, followed by other problems such as population explosion, poverty, and other social, political and religious upheavals. But the poem concludes with a note of uncertainty,

> When, finally, we reached the place
> We hardly know we were there
> The trip had darkened every face

Our deeds were neither great nor rare
Home is where we have gather grace.

Obviously, the poem begins with a pilgrimage which is the ultimate realisation of the exterior truth and culminates in the home which is nothing but introspection that provides inward bliss of knowledge and truth.

In the Indian society the role of mother-in-law and father-in-law in a family, and their relationship and treatment with their daughter-in-law is peculiar, and this has been dealt by the poet in his poem 'Dead-end Story',

Typical Indian Mother-in-law...
Complained
To her husband and son
That girl is no help to me
In the kitchen, is she?
Said the modern advanced bride
I won't lake it.
Either she lets me he her
In the kitchen or she mustn't complain
That I don't help her the kitchen.
Said her father-in-law
You must try understand
Your mother-in-law
She's a very kind woman, you know.

The new bride has to face the dubious nature of her mother-in-law, her backbiting and dichotomy in her daily life which brings family feud and quarrel. There is no transparency in their dealings, and even the father-in-law takes her side who tries to assuage the wounded feelings. This sort of the family is helpless and caught between the mother and wife, and solves the problem arbitrarily but the chapter is not closed and liable to erupt again even at the slightest provocation, as he says, "If you quarrel with my mother/ you quarrel with me/that's where the matter stood/when I last heard of it."

'Night of the Scorpion' is a poem which highlights the superstitions of Indian society: the mother stung by a scorpion one day and the father trying to relieve her pain and agony, the villagers trying to console her and the mother thanking God,

> My mother only said:
> Thank God, the scorpion picked on me
> And spared my children.

The rationalist and sceptic father fails though he tries every conceivable remedy—"trying every cure and blessing,/powder, mixture herb and hybrid." The poet's mother is a typical Indian mother whose heartfelt feelings and concern for her children surpass that of the father or the villagers.

Nissim Ezekiel in his own paper titled "What is Indian in Indo-English Poetry?" spells out thus:

> And I realise now that there is no single Indian flavour which alone can claim the designation, and that its value, too, depends on a host of generative factors which should never be simplified for purposes of praise or blame. It decisive factor in assessing the worth of anything of Indian origin, including Indo-English poetry. (38)

In this connection, he cites the instance of *Selected Poems* of A. K. Ramanujan whose Indianness is nothing but "a complex interaction of psychological force kept under linguistic and formal control." He feels that it is a complex interaction. He further says,

> One thought which occurs to me from this example of English creativity at its best is that there are ways of being Indian which fit into an international pattern of stereotypes. The same may be said of being Christian, Muslim, Jewish or Parsi, American, English, French or Japanese, to mention only a few familiar religious and national labels. What is loosely referred to as the quest for identity, whether a spirtual one or only a number of sceptical observations and comments, may add up to little more than poetic ironies. (42)

These poems have Indian ethos, its realism, mind, food, belief habits, culture, morality, poverty, suffering, feeling, etc., as a hallmark of being Indian. He has become a part of the Indian landscape and identifies his commitment to India as one may locate it more explicitly in his autobiographical poem 'Background Casually',

> I have made my commitments now.
> This is one: to stay where I am,
> As others choose to give themselves
> In some remote and backward place
> My backward place is where I am.

He reiterates his longing in 'The Eliot Prayers',

> Confiscate my passport, Lord
> don't want to go abroad;
> Let me find my song
> where I belong.

And again,

> Perhaps, it is not the mango
> That my eyes and tongue long for
> But Bombay as the fruit
> On which I've lived
> Winning and losing
> My little life.

In this regard, Gieve Patel's remarks in the 'Introduction' to *Collected Poems of Nissim Ezekiel* is pertinent to be quoted here,

> The poet's continued identification with the country in seen to have been the correct choice for him, sustaining him as writer and human being; ending with an acknowledgement that his own backwardness as a man, and the ostensible backwardness of the country, are one and the same thing. (xxiii)

Such a confession and acknowledgement is the outcome of Ezekiel's introspection which is a sort of purgation that helped the poet get rid of pride egotism and assume zero identity of total egoless feature. It also helps him to be a countryman with intimate understanding of the basic fabrication of society with human feelings, and so he writes, in 'A Poem of Dedication'

> I do not want the yogi's concentration,
> I do not want the perfect charity
> Of saints nor the tyrant's endless power.
> I want a human balance humanly
> Aquired, fruitful in the common hair.

The Indian tradition's flavours can be felt in his poems when he prays to be with eternity like a true Indian, particularly Hindu. He wishes to be with, "the sky/air, earth, fire and sea". And in the poem 'The Warm', he surrenders completely,

> Strike a bargain with me, Lord.
> I am not a man of ample means.

Ezekiel is aware of his limitations and inadequacies, and his poetic career is an investigation into his own self which is a kind of redemptive move and alleviating gesture—this mental set-up is as per Indian culture. Chetan Karnani observes in his book *Nissim Ezekiel*,

> Like the commonwealth poets Nissim Ezekiel has been consciously Indian in his sensibility. He has not only tried to describe Indian culture but he has made good use of Babu Angrez or Indian English. (96)

In an interview with John B. Bestari published in *World Literature Written in English* (April 1977, Vol. 16, No. 1) Ezekiel admits,

> A writer needs a national or cultural identity, without that you became a series of imitations, echoes, responses, but you do not develop because there is nothing at the care to develop. (89)

Obviously, Ezekiel's perspective is reflected in this generous gesture. He makes a balance between the traditional and the progressive, and so the modern India and its limitations are exposed which may be taken as a common feature of all modern poems, such as, quest for identity, mechanisation and commercialisation of human life, and other multiple connotations.

In the poem entitled 'Island', Ezekiel, like any modern poet, is in search of identity in the metropolis of Bombay, now Mumbai. In the big crowd of such a big city a man is lost; human life is fully mechanical/commercial here and there is no place for emotion or sentiment. The disparity of the rich and the poor, and the confusion of values can be seen very clearly, though it does not dwell upon the spiritual crisis like Dante's Limbo, Baudelaire's Paris, Laforgue's The City', Eliot's London or Joyce's Dublin. It has, the feeling of harsh and unresolved complexity which appeals in a troubles time of complex modernity to our anguished hearts dealing with the various kinds of social, moral and spiritual disorders. All these feelings have been concretized into the image of an island; that is, the metropolis of Bombay. In this troubled city, Ezekiel is to find his own way. Surprisingly, he does not talk of abandoning the place rather his wish is to indulge in its variety In this ambiguous and confused world he cries for help; he is fractured within and the distorted echoes can be heard outside because the dragons claim to be human; that is, the voice arrogantly parades like virtue and nobody dares to question it. Ezekiel's Bombay is more like Narayan's Malgudi and Hardy's Wessex. Yet, the temptation of the place is irresistible and induces in him the sleep of ignorance; the poet is helpless: I cannot leave the island'/I was born here and belong".

The poet is optimistic in the concluding stanza because a host of miracles propels him to daily business and as a good native he takes calm and clamour in his stride. Perhaps, it is the question of belonging which compels him to be there.

So, through the poem 'Island', Ezekiel suggests the imperative duality and ambivalence of life, and resorts to have a shelter there itself. Therefore, the movement is from conflict to resolution. K R. Srinivasa Iyengar is more keen in observing Ezekiel and quotes him as "the equivalent of a poet's poet." Ezekiel's confession is evident in the following lines:

> The Indian landscape sears my eyes...
> I have made my commitments now.
> This is one: to stay where I am...
> As others choose to give themselves
> In some remote and backwards place
> My backward place is where I am.

When going through such lines we can easily conclude the Indianness of the poet whereas we have a critic like V. M. Madge who presents him otherwise and terms him as "a puny, urbanite sniggering satirist... a sore, sick and sickening gangrenous thumb of Indian English Poetry" (195) in his essay "Pride and Prejudice Ezekiel's Poetry".

References

Das, B.K., 1992, *Modern Indian English Poetry,* Bareilly: Prakash Book Depot.

Ezekiel, Nissim, 1989, *Collected Poems: 1952-1988,* New Delhi, O.U.P.

______ , 1993, "What is Indian in Indo-English Poetry", in *Critical Responses: Commonwealth Literature,* Department of English, Osmania University, Hyderabad, New Delhi: Sterling Pub.

Karnani, Chetan., 1974, *The Poetry of Nissim Ezekiel,* New Delhi, Arnold Heinemaflfl.

Madge, V.M., *Pride and Prejudice in Ezekiel's Poetry,* NA.

Plays

12

Mahesh Dattani's Plays: An Outcry of the Post-colonial Dichotomy

Talking of Dattani, Rehmat Merchant says,

> Mahesh Dattani's pathos-with-a-punch approach, picked with a dash of humour, makes him the perfect candidate for chronicling urban angst. His plays are peopled with city slickens wrestling with issues—in a manner—close to the modern psyche... change-the-world brand of range and impulsiveness, threatens to upset some apple carts... subtext of complex relationship.., eager to understand mind contrasted by informed prejudices... character growing... build in conflict in marriage., collapse of certain stereotypes... prejudice holder forced to look outside the cosy community circle... (*LT*, Feb. 14, 2000)

So is Dattani, his plays, his characters and his mission. He is taken to be a true successor of Girish Karnad and responsible for the revolutionary progression of Indian English drama, as a drama teacher, as a stage director, as an actor, as a Bharatanatyam dancer and as a sociologist explaining various complexities of society. Dattani's contribution is an asset to Indian writing as a whole.

Indian writing comprises a plethora of plays, in other words, playwrights dictate the making of Indian writing. The rich and varied Indian dramatic tradition, the 'Fifth Veda', enshrined in *Natyashastra* expounded by Bharatmuni is enviable to the other writings of world literature. Indian English writing, too, has sufficient number of plays, with a history that can never be accepted as steady or consistent. Going by the remark of Prof. K.R. Srinivas Iyengar, a conscious Indian, interested in creative writing, he is highly depressed at the dismal sight of the birth and progress of Indian English drama. He says, in his book *Indian Writing in English*,

> Modern Indian dramatic writing in English is neither rich in quantity, nor on the whole of quality Enterprising Indians have for nearly a century occasionally attempted drama in English—but seldom for actual production.

In the same way Dhyaneshwar Nandkarni declares in Butcher the Indo-Anglians, "Butcher them (the Indo-Anglian playwrights), castigate them and force them to write in their native Hindi or Urdu or whatever language their fathers and mothers used to speak." We have criticism of the same nature here and there that reveals the disgusted lot of Indian English drama: Karnad and Dattani, the present practitioners like Vera Sharma, Derek Antao, Gieve Patel, Shashi Tharoor, Khushwant Singh, Nissim Ezekiel, Din Mehta, Uma Parameswaran, Manjula Padmanabhan, T.S. Gill, J.P. Das, S. Vasuki, G. Prasanti, Raj Rao, Leo Fredricks, Saros Cowasjee, Suraj Purohit, Bina Bhakta, etc., we find a quantum jump (so to say).

Pre-colonial, colonial and post-colonial experiences literature cannot be compartmentalised in true sense, they are not divorced from each other, rather a continuous process, recording the vicissitudes of time. Successive waves of colonisation have left its vestiges in the natural psyche and national polity, and the near schizophrenic scenario is a colonial legacy accumulated over centuries, pre-independence political preoccupations centered on idealisation, generalisation, mystification etc., available in contemporary literature. In fact, Commonwealth literature has been rechristened as post-colonial literature and Indian writing in English is a legitimate product of our historical and existential conjectures, a genuine expression of our profound post-colonial civilisational crisis, signifying the disparity between the publicity it attracts and its literary quality and ability to reflect our social and spiritual lives. Like other subaltern theories of literature, post-colonialism stands for those who have been sentenced by history to subjugation, diaspora and displacement, empowering the marginalised by retrieving the voices, space and identities silenced by colonial power. In Indian English writing, post-colonial exists from Raja Rao to Salman Rushdie, among several others, in the plays of Girish Karnad, Vijay Tendulkar, Mahesh Elkunchwar, etc., the complexities of post-colonialism being inherited from the colonial and pre-colonial times. Like Arthur Miller and Arnold Wesker, Asif Currimbhoy is critical of values, materialism, corruption, fiivolity, etc. With the reform-oriented movements of the nineteenth century began the major phase of anti-colonialism which sought the tradition to be re-examined; in the modernism of the fifties and sixties, there Dalit movement, the women's movement, etc. In modernising post-colonial tension and anxieties are visible the colonial education, ruthless urbanisation, inhuman industrialisation, loss of faith, erosion of ethos, challenges to the identity, etc.

Mahesh Dattani emerges as a compelling playwright to rearrange the social fabrication and project the post-colonial rhehotomy operating at different levels. Commenting upon such nature of post-colonial writings Taher Ben Jallouin, a writer from Morocco says,

> We have two cultures, it is as if we had two mothers and two fathers, perhaps we don't have total control, like writers in the West, but we have two possible inner worlds, I think we are doubly clever; firstly to use the narrative techniques of the West

> and, secondly, to exploit the narrative traditions of the folklore, the stories from our respective countries, and we have come up with a third type of literature which is unlike Western writing, which is essentially provincial, egocentric and onward looking. We have created literature which is open to other cultures and situations.

Dattani belongs to the section of writers who established women at the centre of their fictive world and may be called Avant-garde feminist. Western education has a liberating influence on women, bringing promise of a new life outside the claustrophobic environment of purdah and other conservative measures. The responses is so eager unselfconscious that are ready to welcome the accident with gestures of mutual exchanges. Thematically that did not desist from the portrayal of the Indian background they offered the gifts of the East in the form of Sanskrit epics and Hindu myths and legends.

Mahesh Dattani is to be estimated on two Counts: first his concern for the fair sex and second his visit to the virgin landscapes, that is, of homosexuals enriches, etc. Coming to his first option, we have ran, the mistress of Hasmukh in 'Where There's a will, Ratna the wife of Jairaj in 'Dance like a Man', Tara the protagonist in the play Tara, Old Baa, Dolly and Alka in 'Bravely Fought the Queen', Deepali in 'A Muggy Night in Mumbai' Gowda and Lata in 'Do the Needful' and Uma in 'Seven Steps Around the Fire. Here we find feminine question for identity, and dilemma of feminine sensibility. Gayatri Spivak in the text of her paper, 'Can the Subaltern Speak?' analyses the question of female subaltern, when she describes women as doubly marginalized subjects in colonial/post-colonial discourses:

> Within the effaced itinerary of the subaltern subject the track of sexual difference is doubly effected.... It is rather, that, both as object of colonialist histriography and as subject of

> insurgency, the ideological construction of gender keeps the male dominant. If, in the context of colonial production, the subaltern has no history and cannot speak, the female as female is more deeply in shadow. (Spivak, 1995, 28)

Spivak quotes female subaltern as "doubly effected", the "otherness" of post-colonial literature. Kiran, the mistress of Hasmukh in *Where There's a Will* and Ranta, the wife of Jairaj in *Dance Like a Man* both belong to the post-colonial era, the "new" women bold and self-confident. Deepali confirms it in her statement "Every time I menstruate, I thank God I am a woman" (*A Muggy Night in Mumbai*).

On the other hand, we have Sonal under strict vigilance of her elder-sister Minal (in *Where There's a Will*), Tara (in *Tara*) a victim of sex discrimination, Old Baa, Dolly and Alka victim of different trends (in *Bravely Fought the Queen*): Old Baa deserted by her husband all alone in her last phase of life, Dolley, a victim of a brutal husband, beaten in an advanced stage of pregnancy to give birth to a deformed daughter, and Alka the wife of a homosexual. Minal's over-possessive nature snatches Sonal's liberty and she is almost crippled and handicapped for the rest of her life, like Laura of Tennessee William's 'The Glass Managerie' and Herbert of W.S. Maugham's 'The Kite'.

Old Baa, Dolly, Alka and Tara are victims of patriarchal society. Going by tradition, women's lives have been organised and manipulated by patriarchy in all ages, all cultures and all countries by establishing values, norms, roles, gender perceptions and idealism that prescribe unequal means, methods and routes to achieve the so-called 'wholeness' for women. Motherhood and wifehood are the dual crowns of womanhood; nothing more, nothing less. In *Where There's a Will* Minal complains: "Even at my husband's funeral, she sat beside me and told me when to cry." Adrienne Rich in his book *Of Woman Born* emphasizes the absurdity of the situation,

> Though motherhood is the experience of women, the institution of motherhood is under male control and the physical situation of becoming a mother is disciplined by males. This glorious motherhood imposed on women conditions her entire life. (p.45)

Barbara Christian, in the book *Black Feminist Criticism: Perspectives on Black Women Writers* explains,

> Ironically, the experience unique to women is interpreted for them through male authorities and structures through religions, myths, science, politics, economics, (p.21)

Dattani's women suffer as a traditional commodity as Tara, in the play *Tara* and, Old Baa, Dolly and Alka in *Bravely Fought the Queen*. On the contrary, we have Kiran and Ratna, emerging as emphatic post-colonial women. The chasm between the two categories of women presents the rift between colonial consciousness and post-colonial compulsions. It is here that we find the post-colonial dichotomy and perhaps Dattani unconsciously hints at the plight of women, torn between being and becoming. The overall impact of colonial consciousness has made us class-conscious, creating situation for women liberation, deepening the feeling of self-centredness and proneness to materialism. The post-colonial writers thematically offered the gifts of the East in the form of Sanskrit epics and Hindu myths and legends, they also did not desist from the portrayal of the Indian background, an indispensable adjunct of their own loved clime. Far from becoming sycophantic instruments of the imperial infiltration of Indian culture and literature, they sought to enrich by contributing to it some of their own Indian and feminine perception of the world. Dattani belongs to the same race. He is like Kafka and Canaus, Sartre and Saul Bellow. Elison and Malamud. His central characters are product of colonial consciousness and they are in search of their lost self, their identity like Blanche Dubois of Tennessee Williams or Willy Loman of Arthur Mullar. As Karl Marx observes in 1853, the British colonization of India had a double mission: "The annihilation of Old Asian society and the laying of the material foundation of Western society in Asia." They brought to India English liberalism, rule of law, individual rights, land reforms etc., as their regenerating role. In their destructive role the British cunningly imposed the Western materialistic values as Indian culture and civilization. Their shrewd attempt was to transform the Indian psyche through a system of education. As Acme Cesaire says,

> I am talking of societies drained of their essence, cultures trampled underfoot, institution undermined, lands confiscated, religions smashed, magnificent, artistic creations destroyed, extraordinary possibilities wiped out. (p.21)

There was a sharp contrast to the Indian tradition that is essentially non-acquisitive in its emphasis, and values but had to undergo cataclysmic change. The erosion of endurin, tradition brought dichotomy in the post-colonial writings.

The second proposition of my paper is Dattani's preference for the virgin field, that is, the sphere least discussed or not discussed at all, such as that of homosexuals, eunches, etc. To some extent, in Indian writing, this comes in the realm of taboo. Though he is not the first to visit this unexplored piece of land, his approach is certainly different. *Bravely Fought the Queen*, has Alka's husband as a homosexual but in *A Muggy Night in Mumbai* homosexuality is the core issue, a team of affluent with lesbians and sodomites. All the characters in the play Kamlesh, Sharad,

Ed. Prakash, Bunny, Ranjit and Deepali fight with their own prejudices and end in meaningless nothingness.

The questions that haunt Dattani are:

(a) Is homosexuality an assertion of individuality?

(b) Is it guided by some conviction?

(c) Does it lead to some meaningful goal?

(d) What is the utility of marriage to such people?

(e) Can they think of a better future?

(f) Does it affect the life as a whole in a positive way?

(g) Should human life be interpreted in terms of sex only?

(h) Is it an alternative to established norms?

(i) Is it a quest for some exclusive identity?

And many more questions. I feel, most of the questions remain unanswered.

Seven Steps Around the Fire, the most popular play, dwells on the theme of eunches, their identity, their constitution and their connotation. Uma Rao, the Sociology scholar emerges as the most powerful character of the play, the mouthpiece of the playwright, who fights to establish the identity of an eunuch, Kamala, during her research on the class and gender-related violence and crime. Its causes and clues, and her social, cultural pursuit finds poetic justice in the nemesis of the play. An eunuch, a beautiful-one, invited for marriage, and the final tragic death—all seem to be a misconstrue. But it happens. The mystery behind the death is there in the police-politician-crime nexus which is a post-colonial development. Mr. Sharma, the nasty politician, does not understand the importance of marriage which is a sacred institution, accepted throughout the globe. The evidence is destroyed but the consciousness remains. Dattani's deconstruction of his own beauty parlance is a post modernist approach: "I scratched tier face, hoping she will become ugly and Sabbu will forget her... She was beautiful. Very beautiful. That is why Salim's wife put fire to her beautiful skin and burned her to the other world." (Dattani, 2000, 41, 15) It seems to reflect the post-colonial trend, that is discourse of subversion and liberation against the politics of hegemony.

Dattani appears to be a reformist, with a setting both traditional and modern, unable to find out any alternative/ solution. This genderless subgroup also constructs its mark of difference, its femininity by wearing saries. As Champa makes it clean, in different situations they can construct their gender and deploy their difference to their own advantage. The power to occupy different subject positions rests entirely in themselves; they create and deny difference, this makes a moment of rupture in the plays apparent celebration of contingency and situatedness, in that it is an ambivalent other that discovers or reveals a fixed form of difference. This gesture can be read as a revelation only in so far as we recognise some form of fixed system of representation. The dichotomy of the play is operative at another level, that is the difference between the findings of social science and the reluctance of implementing authorities. The weakness of Judiciary, that depends on evidence only is also remarkable. The play speaks of subaltern and thus fullils the post-colonial condition of writing.

The most remarkable element which Dattani highlights is the absurdity of the situation in which she (the woman) is trapped by birth. In *Bravely Fought the Queen*, he present the same picture; traditionally bound, organized and manipulated by patriarchy in all ages by established values, norms, roles, and gender perceptions. They are guided by idealism that prescribes unequal means, methods and routed to achieve the so called 'wholeness' for women, motherhood and wifehood being the dual crowns of womanhood. It is the man who was defined this unequivocal terms, as is disciplined by males and they further justify themselves through religions, myths, science, politics, economics etc.

Homosexuality is not the first subject matter chosen by Dattani as writer, it has been dealt by numerous creative talents who prefer to unearth the least explained fields. In *Bravely Fought the Queen*, Dattani takes up the problem of homosexuality of a married which ultimately mars his conjugate life; Old Baa's second-daughter-in law Alka has to suffer the reluctance of her husband who is a big failure in his business just because he is in trap of this dangerous sexual diseases. The same theme occupies the central slot in the play *A Muggy Night in Mumbai*. Here it seems to be a hobby of the elite class of society. Prof. M.K. Naik calls it the record of "Their changing mutual relationship, their revelations, their self-discussion and self-discoveries, though they are all sailing in the same boat each has his/her own oar to put in his/her own flag to hoist." We have a female character Deepali, too, who is an aggressive lesbian. All characters Kamlesh, Sharad, Ed, Bunny, Ranjit and Deepali seem to be of different constitution but equally defiant of the institution called marriage, ridiculing the wedding music in the final Act. Dattani's *Do the Needful* also culminates in confessions of homosexuality by Alpesh whose hope for a better life is ruined for the same reason. Perhaps Dattani projects homosexuality as mode of sexual perversion which destroying conjugal relatlonsnip. It also points towards the post-colonial design and concept that is responsible for dichotomy evident in its continuous erosion of moral and spiritual values and discipline.

Dattani's apparent affirmation of the self's ability to inhabit a multiplicity of subject positions occurs within what Homi K. Bhabha calls in *Nation in Narration*, "the instability of cultural signification" that is articulated as a "dialectic of various temporalities—modern, colonial, post-colonial, native," the boundaries of these temporalities constantly interrupt one another in which the retrieval of the past to construct differences problematic notion of fixedness and essentialness. This instability of cultural significance does not lead to limitlessness of representation but opens up spaces in which the significance functions on the level of temporality whose inflections are governed by changing cultural and social practices. Kirin Narayan's *Love, Stars And All That* also presents eunches, their ambivalent gestures as exposure and affirmation of fixedness and negation of ethnic differences functioning as referential system of representation, but in all the cases ethnicity is situational.

Acme Cesaire in *Discourse in Colonialism* seems to be highly factual in his observation of what colonization has destroyed: "The wonderful Indian civilization—and neither Deterding nor Royal Dutch nor Standard Oil will ever console me for the Aztecs and the Incas". All this results in dichotomy. Colonization brought materialism and mechanism, in sharp contrast to the Indian value based tradition. The perception of life underwent a thorough change—the contemplative, centripetal, spiritual and atemp oral transformed to realistic, centrifugal, material, historical and temporal—leading to erosion of enduring traditional values. That is why Dattani's characters "come alive in their relationship." His cry of dichotomy is apparent in *Do the Needful* where outcasts are agents of change, 'moderns' here are the ones with no alternatives and as Dattani says, "Change doesn't happen overnight, we grow liberal often not because we want to, but have to." It is a keen study of the modern psyche.

Perhaps Dattani's intention is to achieve a harmony (that is missing) through the language of theatre, as he comments in his talk on 11, February 2001 at Ravindra Kalakshetra as part of the Krishi Festival Plays to celebrate the 50th Anniversary of Bengali Theatre in Bangalore,

> Man has created a very complex language called theatre. A language that has the ability to redefine the natural concepts f time, space and movement. A language that goes beyond the verbal, a movement that goes beyond the physical. Trough this language of theatre he has been able to see himself for who he is, what be has made of himself and what be aspires to be. (*JIWE*, Jan. 2002, 1)

His earnest desire is to have identity of our own and,

> ...to form our cultural identities we need all three: tradition, continuity and change. It is when we accept the need for all three in o theatre that we can truly have a theatre movement that is intextricably to the development of cultural, social and individual identities. (*JIWE*, Jan. 2002, 4)

References

Christian, B., 1985, *Black Feminist Criticism; Perspectives on Black Women Writer,* New York, Pargamon Press.

Dattani, M., 2000, *Collected Plays,* New Delhi, Penguin Book India.

Dattani, M., 2002, "Contemporary Indian Theatre and Its Relevance", *The Journal of Indian Writing in English,* Vol. 30, Jan. No.1

Iyengar, K.R.S., 1985, *Indian Writing in English,* New Delhi, Sterling Pub.

Jalloun, T.B. in Interview with V. Naravani, *The Sunday Times of India,* Delhi Edition, Jan, 28, 1996.

Merchant, R., on in *India Today, Feb,* 14, 2000.

Rich, A., 1967, *Of Woman Born,* New York, Bantam Books.

Spivak, G.C. 1995, "Can the Subaltern Speak", *The Post-colonial Studies Reader,* (ed.), Bill Ashcroft, et.al.

13

A Post-Colonial Reading of Girish Karnad's *Hayavadana*

Girish Karnad is the only playwright available today on the Indian English drama scenario, with substantial post-colonial reverberations. The paper intends to overhaul his work in this context with the particular reference to *Hayavadana.*

Post-coloniality, despite all controversies, includes the question of identity, alienation, moral code, fulfilment, mythological orientation, gender placement, metaphysical dualism, neo-colonial dialectic. Karnad plays with historical and mythological episodes to prove his typical post and the like colonial stature. He says in the introduction to the *Three Plays*:

> ... tension between the cultural past of the country and its colonial past, between the attractions of western modes of thought and our own traditions, and finally between the various visions of the future that opened up once the common cause of political freedom was achieved. This is the historical context that gave rise to my plays...." (1)

Hayavadana is, originally, one of the stories of *Kathasaritsagara,* though Karnad admits to have borrowed from Thomas Mann's *The Transposed Heads,* and provides a new rendering to make it more congenial to our soil. The most striking point is the element of indianess, that is, the seed of post-coloniality. It is in abundance, for instance, the opening verse in praise of Lord Ganesha, introduction of *Bhagavata*, inclusion of several Hindu deities and the singing of the National Anthem, etc. Karnad's *Hayavadana* is different from the original story *Kathasaritsagara* or from Thomas Mann's *The Transposed Heads*. The original story raises the moral problem and Mann "uses it to ridicule the mechanical conception of life which differentiates between body and soul" and ridicules the philosophy of the head being superior to the body. On the other hand, Karnad raises "the problem of human identity in a world of tangled relationships." Besides the question of human identity, the play also indulges in the issue of the subaltern it subservient or the other. It is not to be taken at the surfaciel value as an issue of moral erosion or physical gratification, rather an effort at symbiotic relationship. The analysis undertaken centres on Karnad's holistic approach to quantify his progression in empirical terms.

The play opens with an invocation to Vigneshwara (Lord Ganesha), "the destroyer of obstacles", "Lord and master of success and perfection" who "removes all hurdles and crowns all endeavours with success." Yet there is a note of pessimism as the same deity is also described as the "embodiment of imperfection, of incompleteness... with his crooked face and distorted body." By the end of the play, *Bhagavata* is thoroughly transformed and finds Ganesha "unfathomable mercy" who "fulfils the desire of all", and finds himself unable to describe his glory in "poor disabled words." It is language that become crippled and limited in the process of venerating the supreme.

The main plot and the sub-plot are interlinked. The Princess of Karnataka and Padmini are not destined to face the ultimate, rather, they are the consequences of their own options, not imposed from any external agency. Hayavadana, having a man's body and a horse's head, wants to be a complete man; instead, he becomes a complete horse by the end of the play. The transformation of Hayavadana and Padmini's child is identical. The central characters, Devdatta and Kapila, "Two friends there were/one mind, one heart" like "Lava and Kusha, Ram and Lakshman, Krishna and Baldeva, learned lived, fought, embraced and died." *Bhagavata*'s initiative is that of a traditional one:" Each one to his own fate. Each one to his own desire" (11), and then a prominent query by the Female Chorus, "why should love stick to the sap of a single body." (11)

Devdatta and Kapila are poles apart and yet close together. Devdatta is "a slender, delicate-looking person" and Kapila "powerfully built", represent, above all, the two different classes of society, not at war with each other, but somehow unable to accept each other. One is "lost in thought", another in "wrestling", for one Kalidas is important, for another Nanda (a wrestler) is important. They are close but Kapila, preferring to sit down on the floor, insists Devdatta to be on a chair. The conversation between the two exposes this relationship which is astonishing sense that most of the time Kapila is ready to follow Devdatta's request/order only as an obedient slave; more as a servant less a friend; more an oppressed less an equal. The concept of friendship here is that of between the colonizer and colonized, between two completely different classes of society, completely artificial, laboured and concocted. Though borrowed from mythology, it appears to be post-colonial in taste and nature to reconcile and negotiate the two classes. Kapila is ready to sacrifice himself but nowhere in the whole play dose Devdatta exhibit his inclination to that extent; most often Kapila surrenders before him; rather we should admit that he surrenders at every juncture. Kapila's search for Padmini, the most beautiful character of the play "Yakshini, Shakuntala, Urvasi, Indumati — all rolled into one" is not out of nothing; it is his endeavour to please Devdatta, and so he cites: "A poet. A pundit. Knows the Vedas backwards. Writes the grandest poetry ever. Long, dark hair. Delicate, fairface. Age twenty...." (19)

Even after the marriage of Devdatta and Padmini, the old friendship flourishes and the citizens of Dharampura call them a team of three like—"Ram, Sita and Lakshman". For Padmini, Devadatta is a "fragile", "baby", "saffron marriage thread", "deity" and Kapila "an innocent", "a proper devil", "an ethereal shape", "a Celestial Being". The difference between the two is very clear. Kapila's dedication is very emphatic in his several utterances where he calls him "my brother, my father, my friend...", but after the Kali temple episode, the scenario is completely changed—Devadatta rejects him completely, and Kapila's subaltern self accepts it humbly though broken hearted—"so the road diverged". In the last phase of the play Kapila realizes his place and so he says, "I have no place there, no peace, no salvation, I am outcast." (57) Devadatta, too, realizes this when he says, "I wanted your power, but not your wildness. You lived in hate—I in fear." (60) This is how we discover Karnad's subaltern issue unconsciously discussed in the play.

The ethics of human identity and its confusing status is something that is torturous in this play. Almost all characters of the play–Devadatta, Kapila, Hayavadana, Padmini and the Princess of Karnataka—suffer from identity crisis. The astonishing desire of Padmini and the Princess of Karnataka along with the mixed identity of Kapila, Hayavadana and Devadatta baffle the audience. It is simply incredible. Hayavadana wants to be a complete man and for this, he runs from one place to another:

> Banaras, Rameshwar, Gokram, Haridwar, Gaya, Kedarnath, not only those but the Dargah of Khawaia Yusuf Baba. The Grotto of our Virgin Mary—I've tried them all. Magicians,

> mendicants, maharishis, fakirs, saints and sadhus with short hair, sadhus with beards—sadhus in saffron, sadhus in the altogether—hanging, singing, rotating, gyrating—on the spikes, in the air, underwater, underground—I've covered them all. (9-10)

Bhagavata advises him to go to the temple of the Kali of Mount Chitrakoot. By the end of the play *Hayavadana* reappears but not with the body of a complete man, rather with the body of a complete horse and human voice which is further corrected in playing with Padmini's child. The audience is awestruck to find this apparently meaningless exercise of the Almighty.

The audience can perceive Devdatta's fascination towards books and his feminine physical being, and Kapila's fascination towards wrestling and his stout physique; but the mixed identity after the Kali temple episode cannot be explained in simple words —it is a romantic concept and cannot be justified. To change the whole scenario just for the physical gratification of Padmini is not rationale. *Bhagavata* apprehends everything in advance, "And the head is bidding good bye to the heart." (25) Kapila has the right answer by the end of the First Act. "I know what you want, Padmini, Devadatta's clever head and Kapila's strong body...." (38) This mixed body is welcomed by Padmini, "My celestial bodied Gandharva...My sun faced Indira—My Devdatta comes like a bridegroom with the ornament of a new body—It's my duty to go with Devdatta. But remember I'm going with your body." (41) The play continues for a few days but Padmini's "fabulous body—fabulous brain—fabulous Devdatta" fade with the passage of time. Devdatta is puzzled, "I'd always thought one had to use one's brain while wrestling or fencing or swimming. But the body just dose not wait for thoughts—it acts." (43)

The physical pleasure does not last for long; the disfiguration of the physique occur; Devadatta's body turns delicate and

Kapila's stout, Padmini is in trouble again. She rushes to Kapila again. It is not the race for completeness but of fulfilment only. This mixed or confused identity meets its disastrous end. Karnad does not provide any answer. Identity crisis is a deliberate construction and everything remains inconclusive by the end of the play. Perhaps *Hayavadana* has an answer to all such emotional game, "I firmly believe—that it's this sort of sentimentality which has been the bane of our literature and national life. It has kept us from accepting Reality and encourage escapism." (70)

One ridiculous juncture can be noticed in *Hayavadana* where we find Hayavadana singing patriotic songs including the National Anthem. The relevance of this episode cannot be explained and when it is explained by Hayavadana, it appears to be quite misleading "That's why I sing all these patriotic songs —and the National Anthem! That particularly! I have noticed that the people singing the National Anthem always seem to have ruined their voices—so I try. But—but it—it doesn't seem to work what should I do?" (69) The sacred is profaned at all levels, to achieve "completeness" becomes perfect! One plausible reason is the playwright's probable intention to provide post-colonial colour to the old mythical legend; perhaps, it is, as per Salman Rushdie's assertion "that literature is an expression of nationality."

In *Hayavadana* we find a diametric shift in Karnad's critical strategy that we know as "subjugation, domination, diaspora displacement" (Bhabha); as a result Kapila Is marginalized and his marginality is valorized. If the mode of post-colonialism is "the operation of hearing oneself speak" (Derrida) it happens with almost all the characters of the play. As a true post-colonialist Karnad perceives myth and history as discourses, sedimented in political and cultural hegemonies; the empiricist equation of myth with its primitiveness is enmeshed in race for power; it is only myth that offers the simultaneity of past, present and future. It is a hint at our 'national culture' after the departure of imperial power. Obviously Karnad's *Hayavadana* is a post-colonial offshoot of a mature post-colonial mind.

References

Karnad, Girish, 1995, *Three Plays.* New Delhi: O.U.P.

______ , 2003, *Hayavadana.* New Delhi: O.U.P.

14

Dattani's Poetics: A Politics of 'Otherness'

Nowadays communal violence has become almost a routine future that recurs at regular intervals. It has been the root cause of male-frenzy, mayhem and massacre in the history of this subcontinent. Dattani diligently portrays it in his *Final Solutions* and Amitav Ghosh in his *The Shadow Lines*. Dattani traces its origin in the feeling of 'Otherness' and is awestruck to locate this feeling in most of us. This paper intends to focus on Dattani's design of dealing with this terrible complication of social fabrication, and unravel the ingredient of 'Otherness' prevalent evenly across the land.

As we know, our culture relies on collective consciousness despite the surface differences and distinctions of language, creed, region and religion. Hence it raises questions on constructing and reconstructing identities, profoundly. Dattani's play *Final Solutions* is founded on communal hatred, tension and violence, in search of some ultimate solutions. It is a question on the possibility of a solution. Angelie Multani attributes it to the innate element of "underlying sense of 'Otherness', etched into the psyche" of all of us. This 'Otherness' is ingrained in our culture: our lifestyle, belief and disposals. The playwright projects a family, and thereby, like Raja Rao's *Kanthapura*, projects India in miniature; the difference is only that Rao pictures pre-independence where as Dattani's is that of post-independence.

Perhaps such deterioration was noted much earlier in the first quarter of the nineteenth century by the first poet of Indian Writing in English, H. L. Deorozio, in his poems like, 'The Harp of India' and 'India—My Native Land', though he did not define it categorically, In *Final Solutions* we have three sets of characters: the first one is represented by Aruna and Javed, both steadfast in their faith, both reluctant to be apologetic, both playing defensive, both conscious of 'Otherness', 'difference' and the 'outsider', and both having their own convictions of right and wrong (precisely both of them are fanatics and fundamentalists of uncompromising nature). The second is represented by Babban (Bobby) and Smita who disown their communal identity as inherited and religious, perhaps, for a better morrow (yet a bit confused). Ramnik and Hardika/Daksha form a third set of characters, aware of their past and conscious secularist (out of compulsion). With these three sets of characters, Dattani constructs a plot which acquaints us with the history of resentment and ill effect of uninvited but somehow sponsored, violence (termed as communal riots).

In Act One, Ramnik says that he has to protect them, he needed to protect them and Daksha cannot resist: "How could he let these people into my house' oh, I hate this world!" This hatred comes out of the tears of the past; Daksha has in her mind the communal riots of 1947 when her father was killed, and Ramnik remembers the burning of Zarine's shop which was later on bought by his father. This sense of guilt of the past compels him to compromise. The introduction of Javed and Bobby in the Gandhi family is short of hurling a bomb in the quiet climate of a Hindu family. The 'other'/'outsider'/'different', element is brought close, (rather face to face) to the ailing past (Daksha) and progressive present (Ramnik): the past won't surrender and the won't withdraw; this deliberate confrontation is just in order to settle it for ever, as the dramatist intends. After ail arguments the elements of trust between the two cannot be established, Dattani fails to manage the construction of the plot and finally it takes some other way.

In the Second Act, this sense of 'otherness' intensifies as we find the protest of both Ramnik and Aruna over Smita's acquaintance with Javed and Bobby; a distinct sense of respite can be traced in the articulation of the parents when they find that the affair of those 'different' people is with a 'different' girl. Ramnik, after all his pretension to be secular and liberal, nourishes distrust and remains uncomfortable throughout the play.

As we know, neither secularism nor religious faith sanctions violence; they profess principles of tolerance and compassion, respect for all religions, regard for traditional values and ethics, and desire for a peaceful co-existence. Amitav Ghosh calls it "supermacism" in all cases, such as Hindu extremism, or the Khmer Rouge's in Cambodia, or extremist religious movements in Egypt, Israel or the United States.

Ashish Nandy in his book *Time Warp* discusses the role of religion as faith and as ideology. He defines faith as a way of life, plural and catholic, and ideology-following factors such as traditional, political and socioeconomic, which ultimately leads to heinous violence. Here, religion is taken as a pretext guided by acts of negation, such as political creeds and linguistic and ethnic bigotry. It becomes the question of identity, its construction, deconstruction and reconstruction. Thus the removal of the sacred relic called Mu-i-Mubarak, believed to be the hair of Prophet Mohammed from Hazaratbal Mosque became a genocide and brought about colossal upheavals; the assassination of Mrs. Indira Gandhi was taken as the brutal killing of a mother and thus its violent consequences. Similar is the fate of the Godhara carnage and a hundred such instances. The modus operandi of all the communities take a symmetrical pattern that asserts a common inheritance and affiliation, and this avoidable violence, remains a meaningless weapon against the 'other'.

Ramnik's character is manifested vividly in the Second Act of *Final Solutions.* His guilt guides him to suppress his dominant feeling of community and religion; the misdeeds of past haunts him and so he provides shelter and offers employment to the Muslim lad. It is also discovered that Javed has been brought from outside to infuse violence but he does not repent for his misventure. Ramnik is neither liberal nor secular as he pretends to be, and in the Third Act he is completely disenchanted when Javed says, "You have been protecting me from people like me. I am no different from them". Thereafter Ramnik's human understanding and accusation of the whole community initiates posing it as a problem that cannot be solved. Ramnik's tolerance is a bargained one; Daksha's innocence is maligned; tolerance and compassion only become manipulatory tools. After getting instruction from her husband, Aruna goes to serve them water, and after taking water, the glass becomes impure and contaminated and kept separately. In the same way Smita is told to go inside her room. A sort of difference between the Gandhi family and the two outsiders is conspicuous at every stage; this may be taken as the dictates of taboos, but it is there. Respect for one's own religion and faith breeds hatred for the religion and faith of the other. Evidently the tolerant/liberal/secular Ramnik is more communal than Aruna or Javed. Aruna and Javed have nothing to hide and so their commitment is crystal clear. Smita's difference with her mother or Daksha's contrived innocence is of no use.

Dattani repeatedly highlights the pseudo-greatness of Ramnik who is an important segment of society. This is the harsh truth that Dattani repeatedly exposes. M.K. Naik observes that "Dattani is preoccupied with social and political realities in India today." (206) The course of interaction becomes the course of disenchantment in the play *Final Solutions*. At the same time revelation and confusion act as purgation. The trauma of partition lingers long and so is its repercussions; not as a solution but as a natural outburst.; Resentment goes on mounting in the name of peace and conspiracy, manipulation continues in the name of an amicable settlement. It is the lack of political will that disturbs one and that is why Naik calls it a "political play." (208) Love, passion, innocence, aspiration and life on the whole are paralyzed with this boorish sentiment. This is the fate of this majestic land, all against the basic tenets of social ethos and ethics.

We may very easily identify the 'otherness' of Ramnik, Javed, Aruna, Bobby, Smita or Daksha in the carnival of mainstream identities. Each character suffers from a sense of insecurity, of being marginalized, of the dormant strong feeling of 'otherness', and has to constantly negotiate certain role performances, to be iconized as the one 'self' of the narrative pitched against the 'other', bordering on interface with the 'otherness' of the 'other'.

If Javed and Bobby are 'outsiders' for the Gandhi family, this Gandhi family is also 'different' for the two; and it makes no difference whether we use the term 'other' or 'different' or 'outsider', all have the same connotation. Each set of particular modalities of interaction become dichotomous and counter-textualized. Ramnik's hospitality is ontologically relevant, necessitating the spectral presence of the misdeeds of the past. Both guest and host are effectively accommodated by Dattani. Actually, hospitality is all about accepting the 'otherness' of the 'other'; the host should respect the sovereignty of the 'otherness' of the 'other', to ensure an equality of sorts between the guest and himself, thus sustaining trust and understanding between the two. A politico-scientific analysis of the play confirms both Javed and Ramnik as potential threats to the social countenance, and their problematics are structured on the centre- periphery tension underpinned by the different aspects of legitimacy as a fundamental political concern, away from the hegemony institutionalized by the signifier and signified. As Ashish Nandy puts it, "... the suffering of the victims cannot but be the sickness of their oppressors and the intranslatability between two sets of life experiences is complete once the rules of translation are identified." Dattani dislikes his characters to be marginalized or subverted but rather insists an identity framed on ethos and values structured around hegemony, legitimacy and the politics of ideology.

A close study of *Final Solutions* also reveals the fact that every character is a narcissist in pursuit of his own image. In the grip of post-modernist ethics he dwells on "the experience of limits.., of subjectivity, of sexual identity... of systematization and uniformation."(1992, 8) The dehumanization of communal riots is paradoxical and conforms to the essence of deculture which postmodernist culture breeds. The title of the play is deliberately ambiguous, referring to the passion of the play. Violence liberates them, giving language to moods, gesture and glance. Instinct or simple intelligence can no longer be trusted as a guide to feeling and conduct. Probing and questioning continues as a "totalizing impulse", as a "privilege-free, unconditioned experience." (63) We find ours to be a demonic civilization, an animalistic and repulsive degeneration of the human world to the animal world, symbolizing the influence of human action. Ramnik, by leading a double life, symbolizes a major tendency in the post-modern world, "dispersing the will of the one... Janus-faced, anarchistic urge... combined with... a vision of the ideal order." (1971, 100-

16) The individual self in this text appears to be anarchic, turbulent, chaotic and unpredictable along with violence, disguise, multiplicity, heterogeneity and plurality.

Now the question is whether this communal holocaust is the true nature of Indian ambience or is inextricably linked with political compulsions. The dream of coexistence lies in the social implication of constant and multifaceted mutual help and cooperation, emotional attachment and inbuilt insurance against all contingencies. The bedrock of Indian life, upon which *Final Solutions* is founded, is reinforced by factors like depiction of taboos and traditional customs which seem to be irrational and unimpinged by the pressure of 'Today'. The basic mnemonics of this work is loaded with ironies, pathos, nostalgia and duality.

At the end of the play, Dattani remains inconclusive, resorting to abstractions such as belief in humanity. For, in the Third Act, Bobby says about the idol of Krishna, "... it belongs to a human being who believes, and tolerates, and respects what other human beings believe. That is the strongest fragrance of the world." There is no question of sacrileges. Babban says further, "If we understand and believe in one another, nothing can be destroyed". However, the Chorus has the last word, "One reality cannot accept/another reality". As usual Dattani raises numerous but relevant questions: What is the true solution of all the problems projected in the play? Don't you think misinterpretation of the concept of religion leads to such problematics? If so, why should we go back to religion for help again? What can be the best way to eliminate distrust/difference/otherness? Should we forget the past and start a rational new life unbiased and all-compromising? What about the faith of Aruna and Javed? And, how should one respond to it? How does one categorize and understand Smita's love for Babban? What is the answer to the hope of Hardika ("if you call them they will come. But then again—if it's too late—they may not")?

The crux of the text is unsolved and Dattani proves to be inconclusive. The only possible solution is that of mutual understanding, and love and reverence for all. It directly hints at the necessity of brushing aside the ill feeling of 'otherness'. It is this feeling of otherness that creates all kinds of problems besides that of political interference. It is upto our strong will power, our willing to unite, that can put a check on the recurrence of such heinous crimes against the entire humanity. Dattani's poetics of 'otherness' is simply to correct us. On 5th January 1946, Mother told the same thing, "My will is that people should not quarrel... in quarrel I never interfere, because surely both are wrong." Mother envisioned: "No dispute, no quarrels—sweetness of a life without clashes." (2005, 2)

15

The Dilemma of 'Yayati'

Karnad began his dramatic career with *Yayati*, originally written in Kannada and later translated into Hindi and English. It is the reinterpretation of a myth with a novel dimension to make it relevant to the modern world. The present paper attempts to trace the dilemma that is available in both the mythical and the modern world.

It is based on a story taken from *Mahabharata* and its form is based on the Western dramatic pattern, such as that of Anouilh, Sartre, O'Neill and the greeks. As P. D. Nimaskar says:

> Yayati is foregrounded on the concept of responsibility, the burden of responsibility, as the Sutradhar points out in the prologue. King Yayati is under tremendous pressure of the existential burden and crisis and by making a decisive choice forces other characters to remain under the effects of his action. (56)

This play was carved out by Karnad just before his departure to England on Rhodes Scholarship at Oxford in 1960, primarily focusing the conflict between family expectations and personal aspirations as a fictional displacement. It is a story of our ancestors and through it the dramatist can articulate a set of values which cannot be rationalised but can tell us volumes regarding our aspirations, the following actions and the consequences. Karnad is nailed to the past to voice the paradox lying dormant within him, yet he is a misfit for the Indian theatre and has to reach to Greek tragic playwright, Jean Anouilh, Jean-Paul Sartre and Eugene O'Neill for an adequate form to fit his mythical content. As A. B. Dharwakar says in the "Introduction" of *Collected Plays* (Vol.1),

> Yayati is a wordy, didactic, dialectical play, in the style of Anouilh, but it prefigures Karnad's later work in the modernist thoroughness with which it reshapes mythical material, redistributes thematic emphases, and invents new characters to complicate the dramatic potential of a story.... Karnad restructures the story as an ironic drama of discontent; futility and death.... Like the affect figures in Eliot's poem who 'had the experience but missed the meaning', Puru ends the play on a note of stark bewilderment, unable to comprehend the point of what he has endured." (XV-XVI)

Karnad has borrowed from a very popular myth of the *Mahabbharata* which reinforces the counter-oedipal logic of filial relations in Hindu mythology. Yayati is the direct result of his own ill-choice, so to say, which is furthered by the curse and its subsequent transfer to Puru, another blunder in a row to bring another disaster, that is, the suicide of Chitralekha. We may trace the story of Yayati in the "Adiparva", the first major book of the *Mahabbharata* which may be summed up as follows:

> Yayati is a powerful king, and direct desendent of the Kurus. He is one of the six sons of the king, Mahusa. He is married to Devayani whose love for Kacha has failed. On the other hand Sharmistha has intense love for Yayati and hatred for Devayani. Out of her ilicit relationship Sharmistha had a son Puru. Yayati is cursed to untimely old age. Puru offers to exchange his youth for the age of his father. Yayati, eventually, realizes the fact of the matter and retires to forest to lead a life of renunciation, giving up the throne.

In the story, Yayati is cursed with premature old-age for cohabiting with Sharmistha, the Asura's princess. This is a penalty for his highly immoral nexus and Puru's sacrifice of his youth is not his obedience, rather his innocence and ignorance, also out of annyonce for the legitimacy of his birth, and to counteract his feeling of unworthness and enable him to fulfil his destiny as a Chandravamsha Prince. Karnad makes a little digression in his story and his Puru comes back with a bride Chitralekha who has to go for suicide to save herself from the black future.

Like *Tughlaq* and *Hayavadana*, *Yayati* too professes existentialism where he renders the theme of responsibility, explores the symbolic conflict between the archetypal and mythical output, and reinterprets the established values of human life that is called traditional. While talking about the element of existentialism, he divulges to Tutun Makherjee,

> It is true that existentialism was the persuasive philosophy of the time. My attempt was to emphasise the calm acceptance of grief and anguish. Puru's old age is a sudden transformation and not the eventuality of life. It brings no wisdom and no self-realisaton. It is a senseless punishment for an act he has not committed. I was also intrigued by the idea that if Puru had a wife, how would she react? So I introduced Chitralekha. Every character in the play tries to evade the consequences of their actions, except Sharmistha and Chitralekha. (31)

In an interview to Rajender Paul he admits:

> I was excited by the story of Yayati, this exchange of ages between the father and the son which seemed to me terribly powerful and terribly modern. At the same time, I was reading a lot of Sartre and the existentialist. This consistent harping on responsibility which the existentialists indulge in suddenly seemed to link up with the story of Yayati.(113)

Obviously Sartre, Camus and other such existentialists were mentors of Girish Karnad and he preferred to reflect on choice and responsibility, connecting it to modern perspective and sensibility. With certain variations in themes and characters, Karnad twists the original myth to make it relevant to the contemporary world. In the world of Karnad, an individual is a central representative of mankind with an endless desire, Yayati is also one of them representing the endless materialistic desire with a possible self- knowledge and self-awakening eventually. Seema Sunil has translated the Hindi rendering of *Yayati* (by B. A. Marayan) where Sutradhar makes the things clear, "When you follow the trail of the past you're like a lost wayfarer, groping in a huge cavern filled with the ruins of an old unfamiliar mode of life. You grope...and yet you must listen to the call of the past, give it the years of the present. The result is a story of our ancestors, but we see our own image there Sometimes when we are walking along a path we see two paths in front of us. We can take only one road and feel that we are fulfilling our life's purpose. However, we are always conscious of the inaudible voice which says: what would have happened if we had walked on the other road yet let the untrodden road be untrodden and let its secret remain buried? Let us stick to the morals of grandmother's stories that we heard in childhood. This is the sad story of our life." (106)

Like the chorus of the Greek plays, Karnad's Sutradhar makes the intention of the play clear. It is through the myth of the past which helps Karnad in rationalising his organic stuff to present before the audience as a set of values to suit human predicament for confrontation of man for existence. That is why his characters are alienated, absurd, isolated and strangers to themselves suffering from a dilemma of modern man—all reflecting the sick human psyche. This is the outcome of assertion of existentialism which demolishes the conventional set of values and justifies the ways of existence, inviting conflict and confusion of all sorts. It also brings in a dual code of behaviour and moral inertia, giving rise to opportunism, treachery, cowardice, hypocrisy, etc. Yayati is a fractured person who fails to detect the proper meaning and destination of human life; his failure leads him to an insistent longing for death, finally reconciling with the lot of life. He suffers from existential alienation out of his hollowness and vanity.

Factually speaking, there are two extremes in this possibility: one that tells us the undue desire of Yayati and the other is its direct victim, Chitralekha's suicide. The question that ails a common man is what can be the end of the materialistic desire of an individual in terms of sensual gratification. Is it fair to have an endless youth and what can be the possible point of termination of such a wild aspiration? The answer that the myth provides is devastating only.

All characters in the play have a symbolic role intact and to establish his/her existence. In the patriarchal form of society the male members dominate; it is better to say that these male characters determine the course of action: whatever it is the curse by Shukracharya, Yayati's avid desire for exchange of age or Puru's dedication to yield. All female characters are puppets only. As the play proceeds, Sharmistha emerges as the most charming character with certain values and a commitment of social nature and yet suffering from the existential dilemma the beloved daughter of the Asura king and the royal princess with beauty, rank and wealth. She has some rivals, for instance, Swarnalata who calls her a witch and devil and Devayani whose jealousy appears in refined words, that in, not wicked at heart, who takes delight in every kind of perversity. As Karnad himself discloses in an interview, Sharmistha is a complex character and the only character who accepts the consequences of her action, which is the burden of her choice. Her friendship with Devayani is based on high principle and morality but she is conscious of her low birth which brings in ambiguity in her character: "Even as a child I worshipped Devayani. But I was always dogged by the phantom of my law origins." She is proud to quote Devayani as never taunting him, though later on, the sense of cultural superiority assails her and the difference between the two races of Aryans and Asuras comes to the surface. The love of Kacha is also a disturbing factor and the dream of 'eternal friendship' is finally shattered, the two are separated.

Sharmistha and Devayani represent two different races, that of Aryan and Asura, and the differences between the two, represent the existing racial difference in Indian culture, as Karnad has been able to display in almost all his plays. It is not the specific reaction of Devayani, rather, it has been inherited from her forefathers. On the other hand, Sharmistha's reaction to penalise Devayani by pushing her into a well is spontaneous and something which she does not like from her care of heart. That is why, she sits by that well and wept for hours, and submits herself to her friend's social order by becoming a slave to her. Both Yayati and Devayani torture Sharmistha physically and mentally. Yayati marries Devayani to acquire Mriti Sanjivani from Shukracharya for eternal youth. Sharmistha gets a place in the palace as a slave and it suits her because she loves Yayati and wants to remain close to him; it is a kind of pure love for Yayati and Devayani. And this is the reason which compels her not to leave the palace and witness the oppression and suppression of all sorts. She can recall her misdeed,

> Since the day so long ago when I sat by the well and wept for Devayani, I have never known tears. They were ali consumed in the flames of hatred. You let me shed a few tears. My burden seems lighter.... I have finished with the game. (8)

But Yayati remains unmoved,

> She is like a child in many ways. You wounded her self-esteem. Now she counts every insult, hatred at you as a victory for herself. (8)

In between Sharmistha and Devayani there is Yayati, and the two women friends become foes, and it becomes the case of triangular love, Sharmistha bursts out:

> It's a game of chess, where you made the first move. When you turned me into a slave, my mother, my father became powers in the game. After you married, Yayati joined in, and Swarnlata was included the moment she became your darling maid. The people who are gathered there—they, too, must play their part in the sport. And the prince and his bride will also turn out to be powers. (3)

And her complaint to Devayani is:

> Devayani, your gaze is fixed not on Yayati, but on his glory! And you know there is in Yayati's gaze? The thirst for Sanjivani—a drought at the spring of immortality. (3)

Yayati wants the secret of immortality and hence his option is Devayani, and this option is heart-rendening for Sharmistha, flinging her into the pool of restiveness. She dislike every move of Devayani and ridicules her claim for sanctity and chastity:

> Sanctity? You call it sanctity'? The Ghandharva style of marriage! Mating and then asking your name! Who ever wants to know the name of a whore? If you hadn't been Shukracharya's daughter, he would have left you there and then. (4)

Sharmistha is highly depressed and frustrated, and attempts to commit suicide by drinking poison but this move works positively because Yayati discourages such a move, accepts her as his queen and honours her with love. She takes advantage of the situation and propagates the news of her marriage to the king, and passes the news to Devayani also:

> Don't look so worried, Devayani. His intention doesn't matter. After all I must agree to accept what he proposes. Who knows, one day he might treat me exactly the way he's treated you now. Who can predict the ways of these lust-ridden beasts? (10)

After all, Sharmistha is aware of the weakness of Yayati, that is, his sexual urge and hunt for beautiful women which ends in sensual gratification and nothing else. The curse of Shukracharya brings an end to his possible bliss in the company of the king. She tries her best to get it undone but fails to convince the sage. Finally, she consoles Yayati,

> I can't fathom the depths of your misery. I can only guess how you feel. But has anyone ever been able to escape the coils of old age? Why won't you accept it as the natural course of life? Refine to the forest I will stay with you, I promise. (16)

Sharmistha is fully dedicated to Yayati, at the same time, she is jealous of Devayani. She is ready to sacrifice her all for the king. Yayati oscillates between the hopes of youth and the terms of old-age, he is mentally perplexed and Sharmistha is the only one who comes for rescue, and provides fair opinion,

> Why should anyone-else suffer the consequences of your crime? Are merit or sin coins of the same kind, that you can barter them as you choose? Heed my advice. Retire to the forest. Don't go about begging people to take on your old age. (18)

As a woman of wisdom she can foresee the ensuing doom and blames Yayati for the suicide of Chitralekha,

> You consumed her life. I warned you but you wouldn't listen.(27)

Devayani belongs to the Aryan race and is conscious of her racial superiority. Perhaps, Karnad holds her responsible for the absurd dramatic movement in action of the play. Not only that she is the daughter of Shukracharya, the preceptor of the ruler of Asuras, that is, the demon race, he also possesses the Sanjivani Mantra, that is, the secret of immortality, which has attracted Yayati. Besides, Shukracharya can bring the dead to life and can curse a person, changing his youth to old-age. All these have attributed to the formation of the character of Devayani: an arrogant, adamant, shrewd and irresponsible. Her love affairs with Katcha ends in failure but friendship with Sharmistha prolongs and is eventually demolished with yet another attack of racial hierarchy, and its intense consciousness. It is the result of her betrayal in love and the age-old conflict between the Aryans and Asuras. Yayati has proved himself as a mighty king who is known for his conquests, valour and command over the enemy and so Devayani, too, wants to marry him. Both Yayati and Devayani need each other. Yayati is:

> .... the sovereign ruler of Aryavarta. Even the gods have to turn to him for help, when they wage their battles against the demon-race. Yayati exists on account of his courage and his pride.... (1)

Sharmistha is simply a witness, she does not matter at all in the story initially, but she wants to matter and asserts her identity. And it is here that modernity can be traced in its totality.

References

Dharwadker, A.B., 2008, *Collected Plays,* (Vol. 1), New Delhi: O.U.R.

Karnad, Girish, 2008, *Yayati,* New Delhi: O.U.R.

Mukherjee, Tutun, (ed.), 2009, *Girish Karnad's Plays: Performance and Critical Perspectives,* Delhi: Pencraft International.

Nimsarkar, P.D., 2009, *Women in Girish Karnad's Plays: A Critical Perspective,* New Delhi: Creative Books.

16

Impaired Sexuality in the Plays of Mahesh Dattani

Mahesh Dattani is a familiar name to the audience of Indian English Drama of the twenty-first century. Like Kamala Das, Shobha De, Shiv K. Kumar and a few others he prefers to transcend the prescribed social limitations and rove in the forbidden field of sexuality, pouncing upon the less visited space of eunuchs, gays and lesbians. The present paper examines his two works *Seven Steps Around the Fire* (a radio play) and *On a Muggy Night in Mumbai* (a stage play in three acts) to determine the impaired sexuality of certain section of society.

The world of *Seven Steps Around the Fire* is that of 'anarchy', 'filthy lies', 'castrated degenerate' people, 'transsexuals', 'lowest of the low', 'innocent fools, hypocrites and predators. Uma Rao, the daughter of the Vice Chancellor, daughter-in-law of the Deputy Commissioner of Police and wife of the Superintendent of Police, is basically a research scholar, pursuing her doctorate in the case study of eunuchs. In-between she finds the abnormal case of Anarkali, imprisoned for the murder of Kamla, her so-called sister. Mr. Sharma, a political doyen and a minister, is the key figure in the murder, whose son Subbu was married to Kamla, a eunuch, and after the refusal of her admission in the family was burned to death. As a matter of fact, the involvement of a big name transfigures the whole case and Anarkali is entrapped to conceal the fact. No one is ready to disclose the true story but in the marriage party of Subbu everything is unearthed when Subbu decides to shoot himself with his own gun for the simple reason that he dislikes anyone else taking the place of Kamla. Uma nourishes a different opinion regarding eunuchs, tracing their origin in the days of Lord Rama. Her object of this case study is, 'to show their position in society.' (10) She further opines,

> Perceived as the lowest of the low, they yearn for family and love. The two events in mainstream Hindu culture where their presence is acceptable—marriage and birth—ironically are the very same privileges denied to them by man and nature. Not for them the seven rounds witnessed by the fire god, eternally binding man and woman in matrimony, or the blessings of May you be the mother of a hundred sons. (11)

Uma teaches Sociology at Bangalore University and her paper on class and gender-related violence initiates her to examine the case of Anarkali who is the subject of such a study. She wants to elicit the truth from Anarkali but she is tight-lipped. She applies all possible techniques but she comes to know only thing—that Kamla was very beautiful and she scarred her face with a butcher's knife to save her life. Salim's wife put fire to her skin and burned her to the other world. (15) Her husband Suresh never divulges; he is full of love and care for Uma, on the other hand he is cruel and uncompassionate to Anarkali and says, "She is a real liar, as you said. The usual stuff. Hard luck stories." (16)

Uma has so many questions about the origin of this particular class of people, this genderless section of society, who appear uninvited on the occasion of wedding and childbirth, to bless and to be awarded:

> Did they come to this country with Islam, or are they part of our glorious Hindu tradition? Why are they obsessed with weddings and ceremonies of childbirth? How do they come to

> know of these weddings? Why do they just show up without being invited? Are they just extortionists? And why do they not take singing lessons? (16) Then is it true? That they are criminals? Am I making a fool of myself? (17)

So the questions in the mind of Uma is that of the true identity of eunuchs, their genesis and their role in the society. She chalks out a plan to go to the root of the matter with the help of a huge amount of money to attract them to release Anarkali. She goes to Champa with the same mission but she fails. She tries her best. She takes money from her father and visits Champa twice, but of no use. No doubt, she finds a clue there and that is Salim who insists on getting back some photograph from Champa. Champa has the impression that Uma is a social worker (24) and not a journalist, and provides information that Kamla was everyone's first choice. (25) Uma garners the impression that Kamla might have defied the authority of Champa, a wish to leave the fold and so the consequences (28), but Champa refutes her specu'ations. Yet Uma is not depressed. Once she decides to abandon her search (29) but she is again motivated by her Ph.D. supervisor to dig the case. She visits the minister's residence and there she meets Mr. Sharma, the minister, Salim, his bodyguard and Mr. Subbu who appears to be mentally upset and highly disturbed with his ensuing wedding—"I hate weddings. I don't want all this. I don't wish to go ahead with this."(31)

The final scene of the play, that of wedding of Subbu, is the culmination of the dramatic tension and a sort of revelation, that is amazing, particularly to Uma:

> The photograph—a polaroid picture that Subbu and Kamla had taken soon alter their private wedding in some remote temple. A picture of Kamla as a beautiful bride smiling at Subbu with the wedding garland around him. The poojari probably didn't know that Kamla was not a woman. Of course, Mr.Sharma couldn't have it—totally unacceptable. So he

> arranged to have Kamla burned to death. Mr. Sharma simply had to have that picture. He sent Salim to threaten Anarkali and Champa. He did get the picture eventually—after losing his son. What a price to pay? And now he will be arrested and tried for murder." (41)

But who cares. The world goes on; nothing is going to happen to the elite, no question of mitigating the woe of the poor:

> They knew, Anamika, Champa and all the Hijra people knew who was behind the killing of Kamla. They had no voice. The case was hushed up and was not even reported in the newspapers. Champa was right. The police made no arrests. Subbu's suicide was written off as an accident. The photograph was destroyed. So were the lives of two young people."(41)

Uma's study is over. She has come to know the fact but of what use. It can form a good thesis. But this was not her mission. She wanted justice for Anarkali, Champa and Kamla. It could not be so. This is the rule of the world, the law of the land and the fate of the lowest of the low. Dattani raises pertinent questions, regarding the destiny of the eunuchs, their place in society, their role in the traditional design, their exploitation as the poorest of the poor and the ill consequences of the politician-police-media nexus. The history of the origin of eunuchs is controversial, and different religious sources have different stories. Some of them are born so, whereas some of them are castrated to be so. These sexless creatures, they need everything the same as a common man/woman for their survival in all spheres. Then, why this rejection? Dattani voices their anguish: the voice of marginalized/ suppressed entities. The suffering of these people is the theme of Dattani's concern. It is the voice of typical post-colonial literature and a protest against the mainstream design. This play is open-ended as Dattani does not provide an answer to his grave complication of society, but rather seeks the opinion of the reader/ audience. The question is that of belongingness of the marginalized in the society, their conflicts and frictions, their desire to be a part of society of the mainstream, though the present scenario is that of a forced harmony, reflected in dissensions and inconsistencies in the individual. It is the voice of a suppressed section of society that remains buried in the old structure of haves and have-nots. The creation of eunuch is a natural phenomenon and they cannot be blamed for their asexuality. Everyone is aware of this fact, but none of us is ready to accept it. Kamala Das in her poem *Dance of the Eunuchs* talks of the same thing:

> They
> Were thin in limbs and dry; like a half-burnt logs from
> Funeral pyres, a drought and rottenness
> Were in each of them. Even the crows were so
> Silent on trees, and the children, wide-eyed, still;
> All were watching these poor creatures' convulsions,
> The sky crackled then, thunder came, and lightening
> And rain, a meagre rain that smelt of dust in
> Attics and the urine of lizards and mice—(2001, 271)

The second play under discussion is *On a Muggy Night in Mumbai*, a stage play in three acts. It is the world of homosexuals, questioning the significance of marriage in one's life and in society, and the stability and future of such an association. Kamlesh is the central figure of the play, who is under depression for his early association with Prakash and the present company of Sharad. This is the world of gays and lesbians, and even the Guard of the Society is not spared. Kamlesh arranges a party of all his friends with a mission to declare his early relationship with Prakash as an invalid. Sharad wants to take advantage of the situation by condemning Kamlesh with the help of a photograph of Kamlesh with Prakash in an objectionable posture. His sarcastic remark agitates everyone. For Sharad "nobody's perfect" (59); "*Hum log sub bahut besharam hain.*" (60) Deepali supports the gays and prefers lesbians, and opposes marriage,

> I am all for the gay men's cause. Men deserve only men! (60) Treat him like a sex object. Men should get a dose of their own medicine! (63) If you were a woman we would be in love.... If we were heterosexual, we would be married.(65) I thank God. Every time I menstruate I thank God I am a woman. (66)

Kamlesh admits his previous relationship with Prakash before his friends and requests them not to disclose it further as he is going to be married to his own sister Kiran. He has to tear up his photograph with Prakash which slips out of his hand and is taken away to the people gathered to attend a wedding party. He wants to overcome his anxiety, fear and loneliness for which he visits a psychiatrist too. Bunny has an option, he suggests to him,

> Get married—find yourself a nice woman. You can always, have sex on the side. (70)

Bunny is a transformed man, with a better world for himself, a sweet home, a content wife and happy children; for him this world is unnatural and that of animals; he finds sexuality as an animal instinct,

> Camouflage! Even animals do it. Blend with the surroundings. They cannot find you. You politically correct gays deny yourself the basic instinct of camouflage. (70)

Ranjit is in some other world, caring least for the present and finds India as uninhabitable,

> Well, this is the price one pays for living in India.(70) Call me what you will. My English lover and I have been together for twelve years now. You lot will never be able to find a lover in this wretched country! (71)

This gathering is all opposed to heterosexuals and marriage, but they want to have some rituals, some mantras, be it music or song, but some alternative should be there. Sharad says,

> It is the opposite of a marriage—why not? The whole heterosexual world is run by rituals! That wedding downstairs

> will go on for days!—Instead of fire as witness, we will have the sea-breeze.—Either we play some music or chant mantras. (72-73)

Sharad, as usual, dominates and dictates, and say it out aloud

> As my friends, the city and God are witness to my vow, I break all ties with Prakash. (73)

And Kamalesh with his guilt sense says,

> None of you will acknowledge my relationship with Prakash. (73)

In the concluding part of Act I, with the arrival of Kiran, the mood of the party is changed. She is enthusiastic about her second marriage with Ed. All the time, there is a war of words between Kamlesh and Sharad. Sharad calls him selfish and liar. Another question that is raised in the company is that of the capability of a gay to love his wife 'with the same intensity as you can love a man. (84) Bunny says "yes" and also confirms that his wife is "content"; further he asks,

> What about me? I exist too, you know! Why doesn't anyone ask me whether lam happy or not? (84)

Kamlesh feels that Kiran should be content like "Bunny's wife" and,

> I would pray that she would not full apart again. I was thankful also for Prakash for making her happy. I don't think it ever occurred to her in her wildest dreams that we were lovers. She never asked me whether Prakash was gay. She just assumed he wasn't. (86)

Kiran cannot understand what is going on there in the party and finds herself an "intruder". In between, Bunny explodes:

> All right! That's enough of this hypocrisy. Sharad and Kamlesh are no longer lovers. They broke up about a month ago. (87)

Kiran misinterprets the silence; Kamlesh tries to pacify her; his friends call him "stuffy" and "insensitive". Bunny, again, tackles the situation:

> We can never love one another—we mean, that is—All I am saying is that we should all forget categorizing people as gay or straight or bi, whatever, and let them do what they want to do!—you can leave the country, but you can never away from being brown. You are ashamed of being Indian. (88)

Deepali, too, is afraid of all these nasty things:

> It is not shame, is it? With us?—It's fear—Of the corners we will I pushed into where we don't want to be—I too was once afraid of being a woman. (89)

Bunny's assertion irritates Ranjit,

> That's really rich coming from a closet homosexual like you! Yes I am sometimes regretful of being an Indian because I cannot seem to be both Indian and gay. But you are simply ashamed. All this sham is to cover up your shame. (88)

Act III begins with the question of marriage which is "bloody unnatural"—animals don't do it. (95) Kiran opines, "I really wish they would allow gay people to marry."(98) Sharad wants to be "a man", "a real man", so that "he can belong to that world." (99) He comments,

> You see, being a heterosexual man—a real man, as Ed put it I get everything—If I can be a real man, I can be a king. Look at all the kings around you, look at all the male power they enjoy, thrusting themselves onto the world, all that penis power! Power with sex, power with muscle, power with size. Firing rockets, exploding nuclear bombs, if you do it five times, I can do it six times and all that stuff power.

Kamlesh's depression deepens, "I know that have been chasing an illusion. Perhaps the man I loved does not exist."(102) Sharad's response is embrassing to him, "Just because you find me a good-looking, witty, charming, bold and truly wonderful doesn't mean you love me."(102) Everyone in the party agrees with the fact that Kamlesh's love does not exist. On the other hand, Kiran awaits her man, "I feel like a complete woman with him—I know this may sound a little old-fashioned to you but he is so—male. So protective, so caring and yet so assertive."(104)

Thereafter everything is shattered by the guard breaking the news that the photograph of Kamlesh and Prakash has been found by the people downstairs, who came to attend the marriage party and the news of the homosexuality has been propagated in the whole gathering including children. Not only that the society is also planning to take action against such activities and the people engaged in such objectionable immoral activities. Kiran comes to know the fact. The photograph is given by the guard to Sharad who in turn gives it to Kiran. Now Kiran is highly depressed, Ed is frustrated and Kamlesh disappointed. The party is over, Ed wants to commit suicide, Bunny and Deepali think of their family and Kamlesh and Kiran are left sobbing, holding each other. The concluding dialogue of Sharad is remarkable which is the last verse of the song, 'What Makes a Man a Man', "I ask myself what have I got/And what lam and what I'm not—" (111)

This is how the world of gays is shattered; the dream of Kamlesh is shattered and the unnatural and unusual world comes to an end. Actually speaking, the practices of gay and lesbians are highly objectionable to our society and taken to be highly immoral. It also reflects the abnormal psychology of a man/woman and these people have to play double-role, that is, keeping their company content and coping with the moral world as a normal man. Dattani calls them "invisible" for these people can never have a say in society. We cannot call them a nonentity too. Their rejection of marriage and heterosexuality is, to Dattani's mind, to attract attention. This play is also open-ended and it is up to the reader/audience to find out the answer. John McRae maintains that,

> *On a Muggy Night* deserves to touch the whole society and to be touched by it. It is not simply the first play in Indian theatre to handle openly gay themes of love, partnership, trust and betrayal. It is, about how society creates patterns of behaviour and how easy it is for individuals to fall victim to the expectations society creates.(45)

It may appear unconventional as it is in *Seven Steps Around the Fire* which is woven in a pattern of detective fiction. It is an extraordinary story where Uma displays her dignity and intelligence, and questions her own identity in isolation. In the two plays, the common query is what the society has to do with two individuals who love one another, if they decide to live together or marry or otherwise, irrespective of their entity as that of eunuchs or gays or lesbians or anything else. The sexuality under deliberation is that of almost all characters of the play. They have opted for a different life but they are not at ease with their doings. Some of them escape to a married heterosexual life and some despise their country as a misfit to accommodate their stature, so they are not stereotypical traditional gays, but rather a sort of rebels anxious to make their voice heard in the society. We very easily discover,

> tension in a social context, leading to a classic dramatic confrontation which involves not only the characters themselves, but which also confronts the audiences with its own expectations and attitudes. (46)

In simple words, all characters of the play pass through the phase of self-discovery and revelations away from delusion, deception and classic cathartic emotions of terror and pity; they are denuded and they can see themselves in the mirror before their image of hypocrisy id full of deceit and negation obstructing self-expression, responsibility and dignity. It is completely disillusioned world, that of impaired sexuality and nothing else. Kamlesh is the weakest character in the whole play. He is the victim of his own choices, and the phase of great depression in his life is the direct consequence of his corrective measure that does not seem to be feasible. His past deeds cannot be corrected or undone. Prakash cannot be a completely different identity. On the other hand, his old associates won't allow Ed to enjoy a better life or a different life. They envy the betterment of Prakash/Ed and Kiran. The whole association has opted for the hellish world of homosexuality, and now it is the impasse and if there is any possibility of a better world it is not for Kamlesh or Prakash or Kiran. Everyone should suffer. Sharad is the mouthpiece of this undercurrent. He never allows Kamlesh to proceed further. Kamlesh is entrapped his own illusion. The society and culture of India do not allow the practice of sexuality, rather they term it as immoral. That is why Ranjit dislikes India and has all praise for the West where he can have the liberty of such practices . He has been enjoying such partnership for more than twelve years, all uninterrupted. Bunny and Deepali symbolise an attempt to escape from the past world, yet they cannot dissociate themselves completely from their past and so have to attend Kamlesh' party; in the last scene they run away to save their respective sweet homes. Sharad is a catalyst who brings a disastrous change in the whole scenario and disappears like a Satanic evil. Dattani fails to infer anything; he cannot ask for a better life for gays; he cannot put something new in the Indian society. He cannot introduce a new code of conduct. The ultimate debacle is the consequence of endeavour of an alternative better world; and it seems to be impossible for Dattani to find out a better world for gays. His world of impaired sexuality is that of a pervert world, at least, totally unacceptable to the present Indian psyche. *Seven Steps Around the Fire* symbolises a wedding, that is, bringing together two individuals together for ever. In this design or framework the eunuchs appear to be misfits. It is a different thing that this community of eunuchs also has the same desire but the tragic end of Kamla and Subbu, once again, tells us the impossibility of acceptance of such notion. In both the plays Dattani seeks to establish alternative world impaired sexuality and fails miserably.

In both the plays his target is the institution/tradition of marriage, its validity to the persons involved, its future implications and the level of contentment it supplies. Subbu's match with Kamla and the inability the inability to get a social sanction in *Seven Steps Around the Fire* and the disastrous end of *On a Muggy Night in Mumbai* raises pertinent questions regarding established social institutions. The playwright's concern is that of the futility of these conventional norms.

If we take Dattani as a 'historian of the present' as Foucault talks of himself, we must keep in mind that "the experience of the present after all is an illusion, and what passes for the present indeed is the memory of what has just been present. As for the past, it is always recast in the present, and its shape, as several contemporary theorists including Foucault argue more an effect of the present's interest in the past than its cause."(*IL*, 237, 201) To a great extent Dattani seems to be mentally impaired too, totally aberrated and so completely isolated.

References

Dattani, Mahesh, 2000, *Collected Plays*, Penguin Books, New Delhi.

Gokak, V. K, 2001, *The Golden Treasury of Indo-Anglian Poetry*, Sahitya Akademi, New Delhi.

Indian Literature, Vol. 237, Jan.-Feb, 2007.

Fiction

17

The Nightmares of American Novel in the Twenties

I

We have critics who have seen the twenties as a period of repressive puritanism and conservatism, the wave of experiment in literature being explained as a protest, a vast assault on the past and present of America. It is a devastating assault on smugness backwardness, provinciality, and small town values. As Hoffman maintains:

> The 1920s are a decade especially susceptible to the image making and stereo typing of historians, literary or otherwise,
> (Hoffman 1962: 11)

It has been mentioned in *Literary History of the United States* that:

> From the boastful complacency of a boom era in which Americans thought that their wealth technological power and improved economic theories had lifted them to a plateau of absolute security, they were abruptly hurled into a whirlpool of perils, domestic and foreign. (Spiller, Thorp, Johnson, Canby, Ludwing, ed. 1963:1253)

This is surely the manifestation of powerful intellectual and historical factors operating in the background—factors almost as potent as those constituting the background of the Renaissance in England that saw the rise of a whole constellation of brilliant poets and playwrights. The immense literary influence of Freud, Idler and Jung, of the 'stream of consciousness' of William James, and of Expressionism and Existentialism as the novel technique of writers, Eintstein's 'Theory of Relativity', and the most influential Whitehead's 'Science and the Modern World'. The decade was trying to emerge from the shell-shock of the First World War that had just ended in 1918. This brutal war had blown the old Victorian world of optimism and complacency to smithereens. Hoffman explains it as follows:

> The principal areas of critical discourse were psychoanalysis and the Nietzschean rebellion. Freud provided the tools of analysis for the examination of what Nietzsche had described as the consequence of God's death. (p. 446)

The historical and intellectual climate of the decade, therefore, comprises of the severe psychic trauma of war, its effect on values, morals and behaviour, the developments in science, psychology, arts and sociology, the artist's discontent with America and their flight to Paris—the phenomenon of expatriation and opening of doors to continental influences. The strongest mark of the twenties is the widespread conviction that anyone could do anything.

The twentieth century attained its full manifestation in the 1920s through a number of outstanding books: Sherwood Anderson's *Winesburg Ohio*, T.S. Eliot's *The Waste Land*, Ernest Hemingway's *The Sun Also Rises*, F. Scott Fitzgerald's *The Great Gatsby*, Thomas Wolf's *Look Homeward Angel*, Ezra Pound's *Hugh Selwyn Mauberby*, William Faulkner's *The Sound and the Fur*, etc. To the above list of excellence in fiction and poetry one may add the names of Eugene O'Neill, Van Wyck Brooks, Gertrude Stein, John Dos Passos and E.E Cummings. One discovers with a sense of wonder that almost all great works of prose fiction of our time can be traced to the twenties. In the twenties modern American fiction had its beginning in the fiction of Sherwood Anderson and before the decade came to its close, the form had attained extraordinary depth, variety and maturity. Ernest Hemingway, F. Scott Fitzgerald, William Faulkner and Thomas Wolfe were among the greatest luminaries of modern American literature, who exercised their intellect in their particular form of literature. C.D. Verma is of the view:

> Fiction is the most effective form of literary expression, because in fiction alone the modern sensibility meets the needs.(1991, Preface)

In the whole culture of Western Europe, American literature became the major force because the experience of major changes was so much more dramatic in the violence of America's rapid growth R. E. Spiller affirms:

> .... a group of literary radicals, led by Randolph Bourne, Van Wyck Brooks and H.L. Meneken, celebrated the death of 'Puritanism' and the birth of a self-conscious critical movement. It was a time of youth and change of promise, the launching of America's second literary renaissance. (Spiller, 1967: 158)

According to Richard Chase, the American novel was born out of a culture of contradiction. Its genesis lies in "the aesthetic possibilities of radical forms of alienation, contradiction and disorder".

D.H. Lawrence discovers contradiction in the duplicacy of the American literary mind because of a basic opposition between the puritan consciousness and the native spirit of the place; it acquired a new immediacy and relevance not only for America but for all who were interested in contemporary life and art.

With the advent of the 'big three' of the twenties—Hemingway, Fitzgerald and Faulkner—the American novel entered the modernist phase: the war and its terror, as a reality and as a metaphor, outside and deep down in the human psyche, provides the warp and woof of their novels. The novelists of the decade continue writing with another psychic shift: the conflict assumes greater importance now and the clouds of another war darken the horizon, the naturalism and realism in fiction give rise to a heightened absurdity and surrealism.

The writers of the twenties were released from the stiffing restrictions of the previous generation's narrow hypocritical attitudes into a freedom that was heady with optimism. Fitzgerald remarks:

> It seemed only a question of few years before the older people would step aside and let the world be run by those who saw things as they were—and it all seemed rosy and romantic to us who were young then ..... (Mizener, 1963: 6)

A time had come when American writers could think it possible to make major works of literature out of American experience. They thought it was possible to tell the truth about the inner experience of Americans, to describe the way it was, as Hemingway puts it; their subject was the making of Americans, different from the political one, the notion that Americans were new men as products of a novel social experience. In this decade a new passion and consciousness and a new literary experimentalism came into American writing, 'Coming of age', to use Van Wyck Brooks' famous phrase. American novel asserted itself positively as a national form and at the same time took on international power and influence. The earlier American writers like Melville were rediscovered to prove that the novel in America was distinct, modern, and potentially natural in performance and criticism. As Macolm Bradbury puts it:

> We were radicals in literature and sometimes in politics but conservative in our other aspirations looking back for ideals.... (Bradbury, 1980, 11)

He further says,

> ... a period of intensified style in life an era of new manners, self-conscious fashions, explorations of new taste, a modernized world—weariness, a dedication to a changing historical sense of fashion ... of behavioural experimentalism, startling new styles, of personality, attempts at new starts anti the new definition, of social identity crisis—a period highly modern. (Bracibury, 1980; 14)

Fitzgerald's discovery of the tradition of American naturalism, Faulkner's radical experiments with technique, his determination to realize the democratic dream, Hemingway's criticism of the American society, Dos Passos's social protest inspired by democratic or revolutionary zeal, Anderson's suffocation of being caught at a moment of transition, Sinclair Lewis' iconic transcriptions of American life—are some of the remarkable endeavours of the American twenties. R.E., Spiller is of the view that,

> Fitzgerald's strength and his weakness lay in the sincerity of his confession and in the gift of words in which it was expressed.... Dos Passos sought to resolve the central conflict of modern living.... Wolf confronted the same conflict.... (Spiller, 1967: 192-200)

American literature reached a new height of technical perfection and depth of meaning in this period. Among critics Malcolm Cowley and Edmund Wilson were their best spokesmen.

According to Wilson, Symbolism, Freudianism and Marxism were the three forces operating on the literary mind of his times. Symbolism is primarily a concern of art as such, whereas the other two are formulations of personality and of society.

II

Leslie A. Fielder in his book *Love and Death in the American Novel* maintains that "American novel is pre-eminently a novel of terror, a world of fear and loneliness. (p.XX-XX) Right from its emergence it has been in the trap of confusion and dichotomy. That is why Richard Chase is of the view that American novel was born out of a culture of contradictions and its genesis lies in "the aesthetic possibilities of radical forms of alienation, contradiction and disorders". On the other hand, D. H. Lawrence discovers contradiction in the 'duplicacy' of the American literary mind because of the basic opposition between the Puritan consciousness and the native 'spirit of the place'; which forms the core of American fiction, that is at once terrifying and mysterious. This nightmare was perpetuated with the two world wars and introduction of new technology and threat in survival in the twentieth century. The war and terror brought change, shift and distortion in the approach, from and content of the novel; it exercises ideology and psychology pressure and search for urgent solution to the existing complexities through Biblical designs. In the writings of the 1920s, the social conflict dominates and a distinct it; shift is notable in the emergence of heightened absurdity and surrealism instead of naturalism and realism. The Second World War brings another spell of terror and insecurity and there is transmutation in the strategies of survival. To the modern man complexity of disintegration and disillusionment continues as a routine affair where as the present lot strives for psychic steadiness to counter the working anarchy of existing social set-up evident in violence, vendetta, crime, sexism autoeroticism, fantasy and utopia, available in symbolic relativistic open-ended and elastic form instead of definite organic structure. The crisis deepens after the second World War because various reasons:

(i) War psychosis outlives the war and becomes permanent and universal.

(ii) American pre-eminence gives way to cold war abroad and confirmism at home.

(iii) Dissent and division bring about terrible political violence and protest movements of different minority groups, viz., Liberation fronts Warresisters, Women Libbers, Chicano and Red Power, hippies, freaks, crazies, etc.

(iv) The subsequent mood of exhaustion, retreat and withdrawal.

(v) New brands of counter culture and minority culture seeking own brands of survival.

(vi) Quest for identity, survival and authenticity.

(vii) The emergence of contemporary novel otherwise called 'surfiction, 'metafiction, and experimental.'

(viii) Emergence of a new school of criticism.

Lionel Trilling in his book *The Liberal Imagination* admits the fact and says that, "In any culture there are likely to be certain artists who contain a large part of the dialectic within themselves... the very essence... the yes and no of their culture." (p.7)

F. Scott Fitzgerald calls it "creative tension of the artist a the ability to hold two opposed ideas in the mind at the same time, and still retain the ability to function" (Fitz; 1965, 39.) It is this dichotomy that compels Henry James to define American life as "all inclusion and confusion", and art as " all discrimination and selection." (Blackmur, 1934, 120) It also refers to the human life as such, rich in all respects but chaotic at heart, to use Henry James' fine phrase a "splendid waste" and "the only reason for the existence of the novel is that it does attempt to represent life." (Wellek; 1966, 220) Obviously, it is the complexities and ambiguities of human life in general and American life in particular that provide contradiction to American novel.

David Madden correlates the American Nightmare to the American Dream:

> It appears that there are two major American Dream myths: the Old Testament idea of a paradise hopelessly lost, followed by endless nightmare suffering; and the New Testament idea of a paradise that a new American Adam will eventually regain, Most serious fiction is slanted against the New Testament vision: hope for clear vision lies in the ambiguous area between *Paradise Lost* and *Paradise Regained.* (Madden; 1970, XXXIX)

It is a conflict between those who hold American life and values as the last vestige of excellence and the inherited perfection of Eden, and others who came to the disenchanting conclusion that the innocent American Adam and his ideal milieu as figments of imagination It has been a product of historical processes, as George O' Neil expresses in his book *American Dream,*

> ... that marvellous rich silence... that darkness... just equipped for proving that the whole damned world is a zero... well, I am the American story... I'm here fully equipped to revel in the utopia produced by those relentless idealist of the past.... (O' Neil. 1993,125-126)

In an attempt to appreciate the distinctive traits of American novel, many critics try to locate it in its cultural context.

R.W.Lewis, in his book *The American Adam* draws our attention to the Adamic myth of America and points to the protagonists of the American novel as enacting drama of Adamic initiation. Richard Chase, in his book *The American Novel and its Tradition* remarks on the American passion for "the disconnected and the uncontrolled in human experience", and points to the novels as products of this passion which lead to radical forms of alienation, contradiction and disorder. Besides, the multidimensional and pluralistic character of American life provide varying stances and room for contradiction as evident in Hawthorn's 'The Scarlet Letter', presenting the clash of moral, societal and individual values. Ihab Hassan in his book *Contemporary American Literature, 1945-1972,* points out,

> Survival appears indeed both the secret and paramount obsession of contemporary man—the discriminations of race and sex, political protests of every kind—all these perpetuate a mood of crisis that no writer can entirely ignore—the collapse of older values leaves the world in the form of organized chaos, a demonic mixture of order and anarchy. Increasingly, the public realm seems ruled by a variety of fantasies, instantaneous, comical, dreadful —the strange paradox of a world extensively homogenized yet intensely fragmented. (Hassan, 1973, 2-3)

Obviously, the nightmare of American novel is fall out of its divergent people, culture, dream and the Adamic instinct.

References

Blackmur, R.P., (ed.), 1934, *The Art of the Novel Critical Prefaces of Henry James*, New York.

Bradbury & Palmer, (ed.), 1980, *The American Novel and the Nineteen Twenties*, New Delhi, Arnold-Heinemann.

Chase, R., 1957, *The American Novel and its Tradition*, New York.

Fiterzgerald, F.S., 1965, *The Crack-Up and Other Pieces and Stories*, Harmondsworth.

Hassan, 1., 1973, *Contemporary American Literature 1945-1972*, New York, Ungar Pub. Co.

Hoffman F.J., 1962, *The Twenties: American Writing in the Post war Decade*, New York.

Trilling, L., 1953,*The Liberal Imagination*, New York.

Madden D, 1970, *American Dreams, American Nightmares*, Carbondale.

Mizener, A., 1963, *Scott Fitzgerald*, Princeton Hall, Inc.

O'Neil, G., 1933, *American Dream*, New York.

Spiller, R.E., 1967, *The Cycle of American Literature*, The Free Press, New York.

Spiller, Thorp, Johnson, Canby, Ludwing, (ed.), 1963, *Literary History of the United States*, New Delhi, Amerind.

Verma, C.D., 1981. *The Exile Hero and Reintegrating Vision*, New Delhi, Stert, Publication.

Wellek R., (ed.) 1966, *A History of Modern Criticism* (Vol. IV), London.

18

Paradox in Fitzgerald's Paradise

I

This is an attempt of self-evaluation of the works of F. Scott Fitzgerald, confined to the tracing of elements of paradox operating at several levels and its genesis. Fitzgerald as a true "Spokesman of the 1920s"[1] remains "fascinating as a cultural spectacle because the decade enshrines a paradox,"[2] elaborates the constitutions of the contemporary society, individual and the world at large. Sustaining the trauma of World War I, the 1920s felt the failure of culture, entertainment, family life and religion, "failure of communication...of social meaning and value...of morality,"[3] competing them to be rebellious of the older generation, society and tradition.

II

The extent of paradox range from private personal world to the chaotic external world as an offshoot of "evolution of American experiment in fiction, the dimensions of American modernism"[4] As Lionel Trilling points out in *The Liberal Imagination* "in any culture there are likely to be certain artists who contain a large part of the dialectic within themselves...the very essence...the yes and no of their culture".[5] It is true with Fitzgerald. Paradox is implied in the behaviour and attitude of different characters that cease to develop, rather they continue to shift from one stance to another in pursuit of identity and recognition, and eventually fail miserably.

Amory, the protagonist of his first novel *This Side of Paradise* shifts his ambition from being a great halfback, that is, a successful sportsman to that of an ideal beloved, and finally "a man of personality—Big Man". He loves Princeton as it stands for handsome prosperity and social prominence. Not only that, he takes up literature, too, to prove his talent and gather acknowledgement. For the young man who set it down that "if I couldn't be perfect I wouldn't be anything", this, "not quite, was worse than no success at all".[6]

Paradox is implied in his yearning for Rosalind who cannot be wooed with aesthetic sensibility rather than inhuman capitalism. Rosalind overtly confesses: "I cannot be shut away from the trees and flowers, cooped up in a little flat that awaiting for you. You'd hate me in a narrow atmosphere. I'd make you hate me".[7] Here goes the clash between the two worlds: spiritual and materialistic. Amory is a misfit for the Paradise, a paradise that thrives on a dream and culminates in disenchantment. As a last resort, he becomes a socialist and his final pronouncement keeps us awestruck: "Wealthy men are the keepers of the world's intellectual conscience."[8] He admits that he is arguing socialism and the reason he says, "I'm sick of a system where the richest man gets the most beautiful girl, if he wants her."[9] Conspicuous association of wealth, intellect and love is quite ridiculous here. Perhaps the controversy has its roots in the aspiration of the new generation, that of post-World War I that rears poverty and worships success, that "finds all Gods dead, all wars faught, all faith in man shaken."[10] The turmoil within Amory is an offshoot of distrust in religion, faith and tradition that settles on his final realisation, "I know myself, but that is all." Amory's idea of religion, at the end of *This Side of Paradise*: "The idea was strong in him that there was an intrusive lack in those to whom religion was necessary and religion to Amory meant the Church of Rome. Quite conceivably it was an empty ritual, but it was seemingly the only assimilative traditionary bulwark against the decay of morals.... Yet acceptance was, for the present, impossible.[12] Amory's failure at different junctures is described by saying, "The fundamental Amory, idle, imaginative, rebellious, had been nearly snowed under. He had confronted, he had succeeded, but as his imagination was neither satisfied nor grasped by his own success, he had listlessly, half accidentally: checked the whole thing and become again...the fundamental Amory."[13]

III

Fitzgerald's heroes fail to maintain a balance between the finite and the eternity, the viable and the impossible. As a result, they undergo a constant threat of losing youth, beauty and glamour as in *Winter Dreams* Judy Jones and Dixter Green postulate. In the works of Fitzgerald exuberance of wealth governs morality, values and courtship. All his heroines, Rosalind, Necole, Gloria, Daisy, etc., need beauty and luxury, and so they opt for inadequate sposues: a psychiatrist, or likewise. In almost all his works affluence plays the pivotal role in determining the atmosphere of novel that ultimately proves to be tasteless, indecent and inhuman. Obviously women characters evolve as perennial paradoxical phenomenon. In the *Bridal Party*, Michael suffers the same misfortune as insolvency prevents him to win his love: "...lost her, slowly, tragically, uselessly, because he had no money and could make no money, because loving him still, Caroline had lost faith and began to see him as something pathetic, futile and shabby outside the great, shining stream of life toward which she was inevitably drawn."[14]

In the *Winter Dream* and *The Great Gatsby* we discover the heroes with identical ideals revealing the ignorance of the pragmatic discipline of society. Once again, the obsession for wealth and woman dominates that keep on hunting the hero, Jay Gatsby. About Daisy he feels that "her voice is full of money." Cody becomes Gatsby's symbol of greatness as he can buy anything he wants, "a gray, fluid man with a hard, empty face, the pioneer debauchee, who during one phase of American life, brought back to the Eastern Seaboard and savage violence of the frontier brothel and saloon."[15] Goldhurst writes, *The Great Gatsby* reveals the novelist in the act of judging the values of a particular social class (the very rich)" [16] Even Piper strikes a similar chord when he says, "the morality of money is Fitzgerald's major theme."[17] Fitzgerald himself admits, "money is power"[18] Gatsby's meeting with Daisy is "a colossal accident" and he tries to influence her by deceiving her about his status of life. Her marriage with Tom is a display of wealth only so Gatsby decides to win her back with 'money' He is convinced of the ostentation of the underworld to make fortune through illegal manipulations. He manoeuvres his affairs to the day when. with Carraway as host, Daisy is finally returned to him for a while. He parades his affluence to win her back. He nurtures his illusion to the end and dedicates to the purpose of "the service of the vast, vulgar and meretricious beauty."[19] The conversion of the protagonist of *This Side of Paradise* to a naive socialism had less to do with genuine political persuasion than with Fitzgerald's sense of a universe which polarized around wealth and poverty, purity and corruption, youth and age. Later on, with *The Great Gatsby, Tender is the Night*" and *The Last Tycoon*, he begins to appreciate the creative tensions within his own work and admires "the ability to hold two opposed ideas in the mind, at the same time, and still retain the ability to function."[20] With *The Great Gatsby* he retreats from the manichean sensibility of his early works, to acknowledge the crucial ambiguity at the heart of human affairs and to reject the earlier casual moral assumptions.

The paradoxical concept of wealth and courtship results in the waste of talent, affection, desire and intelligence. Excessive sentimentality blinds him to negotiate with the final disaster. Fitzgerald's futile search for 'adequate' and 'correct' modern hero, a man of bright promise, trying to realize himself, contributes to the paradoxical characteristic of his works.

IV

To trace the genesis of paradox, we may go to the central paradox of American history which has been "a belief in progress coupled with a dread of change, and urge towards the inevitable future combined with a longing for the inevitable future and the irretrievable past, a deeply imagined belief in America's unfolding destiny and hunting conviction that the nation was in a state of decline."[21] The duality has been throughout most of America's history and central in the 1920s. In 1914 Walter Lippmann wrote of Woodrow Wiison's 'Inner contradiction': "He knows that there is a New World demanding new methods, but he dreams of an older world. He is torn between the two. It is a very deep conflict in him between what he knows and what he feels, The inner contradiction ran like a thread throughout the decade."[22] Out of this turmoil came Fitzgerald whose ambiguous lifestyle comprising moral vanity and split personality proved a source of "his worst lapses and his truest apprehensions". In a letter to Max Perkins in 1922, he asserted that he wanted to create in his own fashion, "something new, something extraordinary and beautiful"[23] but we do not find anything of the kind as he intended to be. However, it seems that Fitzgerald is conscious of the deviations, that is, the escape of movements of the heroes from his presupposed pattern of characterization which brings success to his craft of handling the characters and giving them the liberty to evolve as free individuals. The credit of making and shaping of Fitzgerald goes to the most controversial decade, the 1920s. On the one hand, the decade is taken to be that of creative talents, who "gave the nation the liveliest, freshest, most stimulating writing in its literary experience."[24] On the other, it is termed "as the era of wonderful nonsense" the age of "wasted youth",[25] etc. As a biproduct of the currents and crosscurrents of the contemporary world Fitzgerald and his characters emerge as flawless representatives of his time, and his works as an accurate canvas of the contemporary world in miniature, displaying the duality of the times.

The American nineteen-twenties are a paradoxical decade, "often defined as one of the most conservative in American history an era of material and business expansion, was also one of the most remarkable periods of American literary experiment, of radical creative exploration and development and the great founding phase of modern American writing."[26] Obviously paradox in Fitzgerald's paradise is the contribution of his times only.

References

1. Piper, H.D., *F. Scott Fitzgerald: A Critical Portrait,* (New York, 1965). p. 29.
2. Bradbury, N. & Palmer, D. (ed.), *The American Novel and the Nineteen Twenties,* (New York, 1962), p. 23.
3. Hoffman, F., *The Twenties,* (New York, 1962), p. 23.
4. Bradbur M.& Palmer, D., (ed.), *The American Novel and the Nineteen Twenties,* (Arnold Heinemann, New Delhi), p. 8.
5. Trilling, Lionel, *The Liberal Imagination,* (New York, 1953), p. 7.
6. Mizenev, A., *The Far Side of Paradise,* (London, 1950), p. 58.
7. Fitzgerald, F.S., *This Side of Paradise,* (Charles Scr 1925), p. 29.
8. Ibid., p. 92.

9. Ibid., p. 41.
10. Ibid.
11. Ibid., p. 111.
12. Ibid., p. 303.
13. Ibid., p.101-5.
14. Fitzgerald, F.S.. *Taps at Revile, The Bridal Party,* (Charles Scr, 1935).
15. Fitzgerald, F.S.. *The Great Gatsby,* (New Delhi, Eurasis Pub House, n.d.) p. 5.
16. Goldhust, William, *F. Scott Fitzgerald and His Contemporaries,* (New York: The World Pub Comp. 1963), p. 219.
17. Piper, H.D., *F. Scott Fitzgerald: A Critical Portrait,* (New York: Hdt, Rinehar and Winston, 1965) p. 299.
18. Sklar, R.. *F. Scott Fitzgerald: The Last' Laocoon,* (New York,1967), p. 239.
19. Fitzgerald, F.S. *The Great Garsby,* (New Delhi, Eurasia Pub), p. 29.
20. Fitzgerald, F.S. *The Crack Up and Other Pieces and Stories,* (Harmondsworth, 1965), p. 39.
21. Bradbury M.& Palmer, D. (ed.), *The American Novel and the Nineteen Twenties,* (Arnold Heinemann, 1980), p. 38-39.
22. Ibid., p.50.
23. Hoffman, F., *The Twenties,* (New York, 1962), p. 127.
24. Ibid., p. 203.
25. Ibid., p. 418.
26. Bradbury M. & Palmer, D.. (ed.). *The American Novel,* (Arnold Heinemann, 1980). p. 11.

19

American Dream in the Twenties: Quest for the Unattainable

In a sense all art is a dream of reality and all artists dreamers of dreams. The dream is a recurrent theme of American literature. Perhaps it was born in the mind of Europe long before America was born. The dream is a symbol rather than a place or programme or precise physical conditions. To different writers writing in different ages it has appeared in different garbs. At times, it is too vague or too esoteric. But at all times it stands for something fascinating, something tantalizing that human beings long for and never attain. The dream is enshrined in *The Unanimous Declaration of Thirteen States of America* of 1776:

> We hold these truths to be self-evident that all men are created equal, that they are endowed by their creator with certain unalienable rights, that among them are life, liberty and pursuit of happiness. (Blake, 1952: 4)

Such dreams are ideals that one aspires for, approaches and never attains. The inevitable outcomes of all these are nostalgia and disenchantment. F.I. Carpenter, while dwelling on the recurrent theme of the American dream in the life and literature of America says:

> American literature has differed from English because of the constant and omnipresent influence of the American dream upon it.

> Even the phrase American dream is of recent origin. But the vague idea has influenced the plotting of our fiction and the imagining of our poetry. Almost by inadvertence our literature has accomplished a symbolic and experimental projection of it. (Carpenter, 1979: 3)

In fact the concept of 'dream' has functioned as a motivating and comprehensive myth in American life and letters, as in the poetry and fiction of the nineteenth century, like that of Emerson, Whitman, Hawthorne, Melville, Mark Twain and many others. In the twentieth century the American dream continues to function as a powerful unifying factor. It witnesses the trends which were then in the nineteenth century with the writers and thinkers related to the Dream. Transcendantalism in philosophy is replaced by pragmatism and realism challenging the vagueness and abstractions of the Dream. The realists, taking the Dream as a psychological force and a standard of measurement of progress, try to find out something real and reason out the causes of its failure, testing the myth against reality. The realists of the twentieth century like Wolfe, Steinbeck, Faulkner, Dos Passos, Hemingway and others have often indirectly dealt with the Dream. Sinclair Lewis turns crusader in his later novels after satirizing corruption in *Main Street* and *Babbit.*

Faulkner condemns slavery, Hemingway continues fight for freedom and democracy and Dos Passos attacks capitalism. A dramatist like Eugene O'Neill, a poet like Robinson Jeffers and a novelist like F. Scott Fitzgerald do emphasize the beauty and nobility of getting enchanted with the unattainable dream. So Carpenter says,

> Many moderns have preferred the romantic quest for the unattainable to the dull acceptance of the actual. (Carpenter, 1979: 56)

And Walter Allen feels:

> ....the lure of the Dream and the feeling that it has been betrayed have been central to much American fiction since the earliest days. (Allen, 1965: 20)

D. Furman in his book *Religion and Social Conflicts in the USA* maintains that the conflict between knowledge and myth becomes bitterly painful.

Slung between the two catastrophic periods—World War I and the Great Depression—the twenties live in many minds as the Jazz Age of Lost Generation, a period of wild prosperity, of short skirts, bobbed hair, of prohibition and bathtub gin, of labour strife and the Ku Klux Klan. It was a time of great cultural change. Till the end of the First World War, the United States was a provincial nation, even, at least culturally, a colonial nation. They believed in the creativity of Europeans and provinciality was clear in the beginning of the twenties. The worlds of Harding and Coolidge, of Wayne B. Wheeler and his "Antisaloon League" of Anthony Comstock's salacious minded censoring of books, was obviously provincial. We find a unifying identity in American cultural and intellectual production that is deliberate dramatization of America's total history. From this necessary and sensible orientation we see the iconoclasm of the American writer as a major feature of American literature, expressing a whole voiced rejection of tramelling orthodoxies, conformities, hypocrisies and delusions. As Malcolm Bradbury and David Palmer maintain:

> The twenties in America remain fascinating as a cultural spectacle because the decade enshrines a paradox. It is thought of as a classical decade of materialism, of business ethics and of prohibition of what the writers who so regularly condemned it and expatriated themselves from it, called "Puritanism", but

> it is also the decade of "the greatest", gaudiest spree in history. (Bradbury, Palmer 1980: 6)

Precisely the relationship between literature and culture is more complex than it appears, posing fascinating problems about the relationship between social changes and transformations. The people of the twenties struggled to cope with massive technological and social change. They sought to adapt to the rise of mass-production, mass-culture metropolitan world that had emerged seemingly almost overnight. The radio, the automobile, the movies, a parade of electrical appliances were still exciting, novelties in post-World War I America. The same stresses and disorientation that produced bitter social conflicts in the decade also made it one of the most creative in American cultural and intellectual history. The unfamiliar and often threatening new social order owe, much to the champions of prohibition and fundamentalism, the trouble folk who donned the white robes of the Klan, the urban blacks who cheered Marcus Garvey, the artist and writers of the Harlem Renaissance. The early Jazz, musicians and the young poets and novelists revitalized

American literature, through the political failures and reactionary social movements, tried to mitigate its influence. The changes, both technological and literary, proceeded hand in hand, as intricate crafts, both became aspects of a single consciousness and imagination. Hugh Kenner defines this connection in these words,

> This means that if Dadalus is the artists patron, art is no miracle but an intricate craft, the issue of which may seem miraculous, James Joyce commenced 'A Portrait of the artist as a Young Man' in 1904, the year after two Americans, sons of a bishop of the Church of the United Brethren in Christ, had flown on man-made wings at Kitty Hawk. (Kenner 1975: XII)

We have critics who have seen the decade as a period of repressive puritanism and conservatism, the wave of experiment in literature being explained as a protest, a vast assault on the past and present of America. It is a devastating assault on smugness, backwardness, provinciality and small town values. As Hoffmen maintains:

> The 1920s are a decade especially susceptible to the image-making and stereotyping of historians, literary or otherwise. (Hoffman 1962: 11)

It has been mentioned in *The Literary History of the United States* that:

> Form the boastful complacency of a boom era in which Americans thought that their wealth, technological power and improved economic theories had lifted them to a plateau of absolute security, they were abruptly hurled into a whirlpool of perils, domestic and foreign". (Spiller, et.al. 1963: 1253)

This is surely the manifestation of powerful intellectual and historical factors operating in the background, factors almost as potent as those consulting the background of the Renaissance in England that saw a whole constellation of brilliant poets and playwrights. The immense literary influences of Freud, Adler and Jung, of the stream of consciousness of William James and of expressionism and as the novel technique of writers of Einstein's "Theory of Relativity and the most influential Whitehead's *Science and the Modern World*. The decade was trying to emerge from the shell-shock of the First World War that had just ended in 1918. This brutal we had blown the old Victorian world of optimism and complacency to smithereens. Hoffman explains it as follows:

> The principal areas of critical discourse were psychoanalysis and the Nietzschean rebellion. Freud provided the tools of analysis

> for the examination of what Nietzsche had described as the consequence of Gods death. (Hoffman 1962:446)

Precisely, the historical and intellectual climate of the decade comprises the severe psychic trauma of war, its effect on values morals and behaviours, the developments in science, psychology, art, and sociology, the artist's discontent with America and their flight to Paris—the phenomenon of expatriation and opening of doors to continental influences. The strongest mark of the twenties is the widespread conviction that anyone could do anything. And here lies the dream at its best.

References

Allen, Walter, 1965, *Tradition and Dream*, London: Penguin Books.

Blake, Nelson Manfred, 1952, *A Short History of American Life*, New York: Mc Graw Hill Book Co. Inc.

Bradbury & Palmer, (ed.), 1980, *American Novel and the Nineteen Twenties*, New Delhi: Arnold-Heinemann.

Carpenter, F.I., 1979, *American Literature and the American Dream*, New York: Armo Press.

Hoffman F.J., 1962, *The Twenties: American Writing in the Post War Decade*, New York.

Kenner, Hugh, 1975, *A Homemade World: The American Modernist Writers*, New Delhi: Allied.

Spiller, Thorp, Johnson, Can by, Lauding, ed, 1963: *Literary History of the United States*, New Delhi.

20

Forster's Preferences and Obsessions

Most often, Forster is accused of his preferences for homosexuality, widely prevalent in his work; it is also diagnosed that it is the weakness that spoils all his ideology and perhaps this weakness became so explicit in to V.S. Naipaul that he rejected his evaluation of Indian culture. This paper is an attempt to trace the element of homosexuality and its ill effect on his ideology of liberal humanism.

It begins with Forster's fascination towards Greek sensibility and Hellenic predilections which argue that man can experience a nobler, deeper harmony of body and soul that women have never guessed; it is the mainstay of Athenian society. That is why Forster justifies the homosexuals and calls them 'martyrs of the law'. Maurice is the more convincing work in this respect where Clive and Maurice approach homosexuality as a Hellenic predilection; similar is the case with Stephen Wenham (*The Longest Journey*). The traumatic years of the First World War saw the collapse of values and his daunting shift to the social pressure against homosexual disclosures, all defying the aesthetics of Forster. His definition of friendship leads to the misconceptions of physical relationship between man and man, and so could never present a successful conventional marriage which goes for heterosexuality, for, instance, those of Lucy Honeychurch and George Emerson, Lilia and Gino, Margaret Schlegel and Mr.

Wilcox, Rickie and Agnes etc. Actually Maurice stands as a confessional novel of the author himself, acceptance of his own homosexuality where he seeks public recognition of homosexuals. Its acceptance was embarrassing to the Forster readers and admirers. Lytton Strachey called the book a 'diseased' and 'beastly' book. Forster defends his proposition when he says, "I was trying to connect and use all the fragments I was born for." Maurice is sensitive with poor self-confidence like Rickie, Lucy and Philip, the early protagonists, but he is philistine and easily muddled, that is why the sudden departure of George appears to be betrayal to him and consequently there is the semi-erotic dream, laying for solitude, afraid of the dark and average. Maurice resembles Forster and his Cambridge is the same as his own whether it is the *Cambridge of Maurice* or *The Longest Journey*. To further aggravate the situation Forster creates an eunuch in a 'rotten style'. He develops friendship between Maurice and Clive on the same line and eases the relationship with the help of Plato's *Symposium*, connecting idealism and brutality body and soul, and rationalizing their physical relationship. Maurice acknowledges his homosexuality discards his superficial religion and abandons normal life; yet the understanding between the two does not last long, because outside Cambridge the world is hostile, realistic and responsible; it has more obligations, liability and other sensible work, call it politics, economic compulsions or social ethics. Forster deliberately makes Clive heterosexual which is disturbing to Maurice but soothing to Clive. Homosexuality and heterosexuality are put together in the life of Clive to explain the details of the-two perspectives. Ada symbolises a midpoint between his old and new desires, that of Maurice and a woman. Clive represents the country gentry, suicidal to the ruling class, as an omen for the future and a fatal flaw in the owner's character.

To Forster idealism is irritating; he doesn't know how to put it, how to make compromises and so it becomes a disease of consciousness. Characters guarding against fate ask for a sort of order and stability. Clive's role is catalytic in Maurice's sexual development and he is finished early. Maurice finds an alternative in Alec Scudder, the final salvation, though he has potentially destructive vitality and animality; and their copulation attains perfection and understanding of the upper-class. Maurice and the under-gamekeeper Alec offending the social and sexual taboos of Edwardian society; then follows the sense of guilt of Maurice, of violating the code of his class. The subsequent revolt of Alec reveals his class consciousness, of the feeling of belonging to a self-condemned class and Maurice stands guilty less sexual than social, 'against the whole world'. 'Sentimentality and lust', 'idealism and brutality' are brought together to definer love; love becomes sexuality and sexuality altogether different from Platonic love; a new psychic equilibrium is established, "In a way they were one passion" (233); an extraordinary psychological conviction is approached. The ending of the novel is 'clumsy and impossible' and Forster calls it imperative, bringing Maurice and Alice together roaming in the greenwood, the fate of the England middle class, a largely sterile and class-ridden society, of communion and communications, of social negation, spiritual locus and vital vision.

On the other hand, homosexuality brings divorce between the inner and outer life, the break between the private and the public actions. Forster's ethics allow fusion as potentiality which leads to homosexuality as 'flesh educating the spirit' (151), sexual satisfaction with the continuity of comradely affection and critics find a kind of penetration into self-knowledge despite the hypocrisies of his tribe and a recognition of upper middle-class life. In *Abinger Harvest* Forster says:

> English writers are hampered because they cannot write freely about sex.... Sex is a subject of serious treatment and also for comic treatment; this latter aspect is usually ignored. (81)

In a way he justifies the practice of homosexuality and presents them as martyrs to law of the land. Like D.H. Lawrence be presumes to be "prophetic vitalist opposed to machine age", "a passage haunted by Christianity" but pleaded for "spontaneity in sexual and personal relations", taking universe as an echo of intimations of spiritual realities—yet in his created world, all these prove futile at the end of the day—because, whatever arguments may be forwarded, this is a sort of, embracing of animalism. That is why he creates models of imperfections in the name of search of perfection, like Philip, Rickie, Maurice, Alce, Schiegles and Wilcoxes. Like Virginia Woolf, he takes the homosexuality and insensitivity of the middle class and finds personal relationship as an escape and alternative. His muddled mind could create muddled theme out of muddled relations, and it makes everything complex. This clash of contrary makes his work inconclusive, ambiguous and chaotic. He sticks to humanism which breeds personal relationship, democratic social attitude and a uniform pattern of spiritual values.

All the time, there is a clash in his work, because the clash goes within the mind of Forester himself, the clash may be because of irregular marriages or hypocritical social design or repressed impulses. Consequently, *Where Angels Fear to Tread* faces failure in marriage, collapse of middle class values and intellectual snobbery: Lilia's marriage is aborted and enthusiasm of freedom discouraged; the characters of morality fail such as Mrs. Honrychurch, Mrs. Wilcox, Mrs. Moore, Mrs. Failings, Mrs. Herriton, etc. The clash between Sawston and Italy is that between morality and sexuality, duty and joy, order and disorder. He hates Sawston and its middle class because of its morality and calls it hypocrisy; in Italy he finds freedom of sexuality and so it is preferable. Gino represents exuberance and enjoyment of Italy and as the ethical embodiment of Forster's primitive ideal, natural but brutal. How to save one's inner integrity and one's face are the pertinent questions throughout the novel, yet the moral cannot be developed successfully.

The Longest Journey is taken to be spiritual biography of Forster and in Rickie's academic career at Cambridge he pours his own story, in metaphor, no doubt, talking of homosexuality inherited from father and not disclosed to mother because of its being a social taboo. Obviously, in doing so, he pollutes Cambridge and the English society with its statement, crisis and resolution in his own way. But Forster cannot nourish Rickie for long; in him, he generates the clash between friendship and marriage, and this, once again, is the Freudian impulse, and the moral and artistic resonance, and Rickie goes to pieces. Forster prefers Cambridge because it encourages and fosters male friendship and excludes heterosexual love, so it is more a battle of sex and less a battle for truth. Rickie is torn between the demand of conventional world, that of a "double son, a loving husband and a responsible father", and the present urge of latest homosexuality in his relationship with Ansell. In Agnes he does not see a good wife, as a result, Ricki's marriage is a failure. Rickie cannot be brutal and dominating that Agnes want him to be; this is Forster's horrible unfair marriage, designed to suffer and foreseen by Ansell long before it could happen; in Ansell Forster has created the moral conscience of the novel and it also reflects Forster's moral conscience which cautions him to behave properly. Actually Ansell feels that Rickie's marriage is the result of the sexual jealousy of Agnes and hatred of the female sex, bound to collapse.

Forster creates Stephen as antithesis of Rickie who is 'unified in body and soul' (94); he stands for the ideal of salvation through nature. The contrast between Rickie and Stephen is the paradox that lies within Forster himself, because he is the creator of both, one to be condemned and the other to be embraced. Forster deliberately brings catastrophe to Rickie—the bookish, the theoretical and the puritan—within the definition of the 'ideal', turned against Stephen—earthly, good natured, ill-educated coarse, non-intellectual with a vengeance, impulsive, spontaneous and rude. The failure of Rickie is the failure of Forster's deep seated ideology and the applause of Stephen is the search of an alternative. Rickie is a misfit as he misjudges Stephen, Agnes, Ansell and the rest of the world. Consequently, Agnes becomes a subjective idol, Stephen, a bastard and Ansell non-entity; to Forster Ansell and Stephen are individualists and humanists.

The central part of *The Longest Journey* is the indictment of the middle class, their assertion of strong economy in Public School, their worship of success and belief in personal influence; and so Herbert displeases Forster, "he had but one test of things success: success for the body in this life and for the soul in the life to come."(194) Forster denies the traditional values and so is Rickie and the reason is obvious, it won't allow perversion in the name of modernity, humanism and democracy. For this reason why he has created suffocating Sawston: enclosed, spiritually muddled and unrealistic, yet self-sufficient. Rickie's love Agnes dies an untimely death; Ansell begins to dominate. Subsequently, Rickie is made to be disillusioned and the middle-class social code and discipline is termed by Forster a social taboo and unrealistic. Forster toys with the characters who speak his own rational norm and atmosphere. Ansell's moral outburst is also termed as unrealistic, rhetoric, "passionate for satire and truth", and conscious of "holiness of heart's imagination." (212) Mrs. Failing reflects the ambivalent character of Forster, a complicated character, full of dualism: vindictive and generous, sympathetic and cruel, intelligent and cold.

Frankly speaking, every new day brings, a new experience and this novelty is a clean departure from the day; people call it novice, a new beginning, a moment of rebel and different from the day spent. Forster also feels that he is beginning something new by divorcing the past, but the fact of the matter is that in bringing the new he fails miserably, he becomes a pervert and he creates a world to his own satisfaction and, happiness, otherwise known as 'Swantah Sukhay' (art for one's own pleasure) in Sanskrit; that is why he says, "Habits and sex may change with new generation" (292), whereas the fact is that man changes but his basics remain the same, call it habit or sex. Forster's definition of complete man is distorted; he creates half-man, be it Rickie, be it Stephen; if Stephen is a social outcast, Rickie is also not all acceptable — he is a failure, unable to meet a challenge. The triumph of the elemental qualities of Stephen and death of Rickie's conviction is the disfiguration of Forster. Robert is another natural man in the novel who rejects the Christian antithesis between the sensual and the spiritual, and believes in the triumph of love — he is, again, Forster's own projection who call lovers as "forces of nature" (238) like Stephen's contempt for religion. At the death of Rickie, Forester's humanism wins and is established; it is not reverence for life, but a trick to save Stephen which can never win a clear reckoning of a reader. Forster has an undeveloped heart and so in describing homosexuality he could not provide an entirely convincing account of perfect harmony between the mind and body, the wisdom of the two and is in search of an elusive ideal, never to be achieved. His definitions of marital happiness fail because his erotic preconceptions are not acceptable to the social arena.

Finally, Forster remains inconclusive, not because of his pretentious philosophy of liberal tradition but because of the reason that he has no specific message; he makes everything confusing and mysterious. He rejects the existence of absolute values, theological dogmas of the middle ages and Christian discipline not because of his strong convictions but it is something given by the generation to which he belongs, which is why it is his notional success only. He stands in a row with Goldsworthy Lowes Dickenson, Walt Whitman and Edward Carpenter who had to make public apologies for homosexuality; it is not only a social taboo but also a virus which could destroy all his work. Homosexuality is natural for them, a natural instinct and the origin of *Maurice* lies in his acceptance of homosexuality, an appeal for the public recognition, termed as 'masterbatory fantasy.' He justifies the homosexuals as martyrs and cites scriptural support from the instance of David and Jonathan and the disciple whom Jesus loved. He calls it spontaneity in sexual and personal relations, and creates his fictional world on a contrast between the natural and social world; he finds that obedience to blood beat results in a richer and more complex fulfilment than a gratification of social desire. In fact, his works are purely autobiographical and in justification of the perverted sexuality, he is trying to gratify his own self, his own soul. His awareness of Paganism emphasise the enjoyment of body and yet he admires Wilcoxe's, who are sexually deficient. He tries to show that sexual perversion is a reality of the upper middle class, but his presentation of hypocrisy is ill defined and so his justification becomes a personal one; it is his private stream.

References

Forster, E.M., 1908, *A Room with a View*, London: Edward Arnold,

______ ., 1908, *The Hill of Devi*, London: Edward Arnold.

______ ., 1905, *Where Angles Fear to Tread*, London: Edward Arnold.

______ ., 1907, *The Longest Journey*, London: Edward Arnold.

______ ., 1910, *Howard End*, London: Edward Arnold.

______ ., 1971, *Maurice*, London: Vikas.

______ ., 1927, *Aspects of the Novel*, London: Edward Arnold.

______ ., 1936, *Abinger Harvest*, London: Edward Arnold.

21

Forster's Article of Faith

In *Abinger Harvest* Forster admits that he is a 'child of unbelief' (100) who is reflected in his rejection of Christianity, Freud, Marx, etc., this may lead to the presumption that Forster is a sceptic or disbeliever. On the contrary, this paper is an attempt to establish Forster as a fanatic, entrapped in his own world of values and patterns, of 'no, not, nothing', and his own religion and God.

Both his fictional and non-fictional writings confirm this fact, Right from the beginning, in his first novel, *Where Angels Fear to Tread*, he puts in an irregular marriage whose ill-effects on the relationships brings about a clash between the world of conventional morality and the natural humanistic world; and thereby the failure of love in its various manifestations, for instance, the maternal affectation of Lilia and Mrs. Herriton, the spiritual love for Caroline, sexual love of Lilia and Gino, paternal love of Gino for his child, etc. The world of this novel is a deliberate construct to prove the author's point of view. In *Art for Art's Sake* he is of the view that a man can never achieve harmony with his surroundings and he says, "The future of our race is in this direction, more unpleasant that we care to admit and it has sometimes seemed to me that its best chance lies through apathy, uninventiveness and inertia." (100)

'Liberal' is the sole credit that goes to Forster most often and then come his policy of 'connecting' under the most articulate slogan of 'human relationship' and love. In *D'Etre of Criticism*, he writes "We must come back to love." (131) In *A Room with a View* he says, "It isn't possible to love and part. You will wish that it was. You can transmute love, ignore it, muddle it, but you can never pull it out of you." (237)

Besides his views on the human aspect of culture and civilization, his exemplary opinion about religion, be it Christianity or Hinduism, or Buddhism or Islam, are astonishing. He rejects Christianity because it prescribes a moral system and not an integrated view of life; not only that, he found a nexus between religion and rise of capitalism. In *Two Cheers for Democracy* he says, "such influences as it retains in modern society is due to the money behind it, rather to its spiritual appeal." (84) Perhaps it is the non-Christian within him that compels him to delineate the Greek God Pan and the Hindu God Krishna.

Most of the time Forster behaves like a prophet, and although he debunks Christianity as a moral system, he tries to preach as a prophet, pleading for right conduct, human behaviour and love for all; the watchwords of his humanism are order, restraint and discipline. He voices the middle class, its values and its criticism; he felt disturbed by the lower class for the erosion of values and culture. In *Abinger Harvest* he cites the characteristics of the middle class as "solidity, caution, integrity, efficiency and lack of imagination" (13); his chief concern is the decay of middle class that is evident in hypocrisy, class distinction and vanity. The finest achieving of liberalism is reflected in civilization which in the present age is based on reason rejecting theology and imagination; agnostics or pantheist being its chief exponents. Forster, however, wanted reconciliation between the reason and imagination. He says that the Englishmen's fear is that of emotion because they have an undeveloped heart which leads to the confused complexity of human character. He feels that human life can be enriched by order, culture and tolerance. In his attempt to bring reconciliation he brings in conflict of reason and passion in his novels.

His non-fiction raises pertinent questions. In *Does Culture Matter?*, the question of culture is raised during the war, its preservation and fostering. He wanted to maintain the culture intact and so did not favour the revolution of the West and the fascism or Communism. He had become a touchstone of a particular set of values and attitudes, a symbol of liberal and sceptical humanism which his critics call a force of conservatism. He ridicules snobbishness and philistinism in a satirical vain as an artist. He prefers nature and condemns industrialization because of its ill consequences.

He sticks to personal values and detests commercialism and science which are for the body only and not for the soul; it may breed spiritual ills, and not wisdom and happiness. In the same book he says, "If you drop traditional culture you lose your chance of connecting work and play, and creating a life which is all of a piece." (103) The liberal intellectuals had a paradoxical position in Britain who believed in government regulation of the economy but not in the laissez-faire of the spirit, almost a Victorian literary enterprise. Forster's attitude is shaped by the Greek view of life which advocates for the proportion or harmony or balance, of the inner and the outer, the body and the soul, the aesthetic and the ethical, the pagan and the primitive.

Forster is aware of the social incongruities and falsities of social conventions which desiccated English middle class life. The aridity of superficial culture and its judgement of what are spontaneous, instinctive and sincere irritated him. He was of the view that all clash arises from actions determined by character, from human incapability and differences arise from nature in its simplicity, and overlaid by maxims or prejudices; he represents the old channel, the traditional one, a bourgeois, calm-intelligible, anti-apocalyptic, anti-heroism and anti-individual. Forster is caught between the two extremes and his novels suffer from contradictions and no final solutions, for instance, the love-hate attitude towards his protagonists and the paradox of being human. His temperament is in favour of a humanistic approach, personal relationship, democratic social set-up and the necessity to look across the frontiers of class races, nations and borders.

Where Angels Fear to Tread, his first novel, is a novel of questioning—to the middle class—and the consequent disillusionment. The clash of two cultures, that of Sawston and Monteriano, that is, of England and Italy, is the clash between hypocrisy and sincerity, the "world of conventional morality and the world more akin to nature", morality and sexuality, duty and desire, order and disorder, the rich and the poor, the high and the low, the North and the South, the cold and the warm. Forster stands for primitive ideal which is natural and elemental, though brutal at times, yet the relationship between Lilia and Gino is imperfect. To a great extent, Philip represents Forster; he is a cultivated and intelligent youth, enchanted with the knowledge of the history of Italy, cynical of his inadequacies, conscious of his inertia, neither a hypocrite nor an opportunist, the archetype of an unheroic hero (of modern fiction), morally crippled, a disengaged aesthetic to whom life is a spectacle, a despising mediocrity and completely disillusioned as the first step in education. Gino is rather disorganized, unquestionably shocking mess.

The novel progresses from aesthetic detachment to involvement with life; shocks and reveals a process of self-discovery. Like Forster Philip feels for art and beauty, laugh at Sawston's pretensions, detached himself from the world around him to understand it and involved him with others, has ethical and aesthetic idealism, and has desire for some transcendent expression of truth and beauty. In *The Longest Journey* there is a clash between Forster's ethical and aesthetic impulses, between his assertions of art as a redemptive device versus art as a dramatization of experience. It is an anti-domestic novel and taken as spiritual biography of Forster. It is the details of his Cambridge life where truth is pursued intellectually, which stands for ethics of inquiry, of open-mindedness and zeal for truth; it also stands for its humanistic approach and climate. Throughout the novel, friendship stands against marriage because it is friendship which paves the way towards true understanding; it is idealistic, intellectual and free.

Manipulation and lie are the sins that Forster places as grim and uncompromising which results in the punishment of Rickie and indictment of the English middle class. Sawstonian attitude is to worship success, not truth; it prefers personal influence and not personal relations. At the same time, tradition is of paramount importance to Rickie, because he feels that the awareness of the tradition keeps us close to the past but Sawston remains an enclosed and self-sufficient world where spiritual muddle and unreality thrive like anything. Ansell wants to reshape Rickie's ethics, and the mode is to bring back to reality and resurrect the spirit, in order to rescue him from Agnes, to understand what is good, and to learn the values in real terms.

Forster believes in connecting which is found explicitly in *Howards End*; it believes in connecting past with the future, the mind with the body and the human with the natural—these things are essential for the continuation of human life in totality —life, death, past, present and future being an integral part. Rickie has to sacrifice his life because he is a visionary idealist. All characters—Rickie, Stephen, Herbert and Ansell—are incomplete. His *The Longest Journey* has the elements of Greek tragedy like Ibsen's *Ghosts* (in interaction with the past and present) where heroes define an opposing world which is full of lies and compromises, and dead positions. They have to struggle against all the odds because they discover that man belongs to this world and have its destructive inheritance in themselves; finally Rickie stands for the disintegration of personality.

Forster studies the modern life as the Greeks did and so he insists on "a return to the Greek ideal of beauty as a penance for all ills of modern life." He does not go but the Christian outlook but divides people into animal and rational, but he does not follow the Greek and Latin religious mythology. Stephen is established as heroic, and all through the novel we find man's double relationship with divinity as in Genesis: Rickie, Agnes and Mrs. Failing who constitute a trio which reminds us of the trio of Adam, Eve and Satan where Mrs. Failing represents Satan, Rickie is Adam and Agnes is Eve. There is an extremely dense clash of vision, with conscious intelligence and resolution; it emerges as a meditation on the dangers and attractions of romanticism where adjustment with reality proves to be a radical failure. All his novels conclude in retreat and withdrawal; his antipathy to the modern world brings him back to the countryside, the extraordinary rural world—it is reflected in the search of Rickie which again brings the clash of inner life and outer life, real and unreal, sexual and spiritual, conventional and modern, intellectual and physical, body and mind—but Forster wants to bridge the gap between these twos.

In the overtly romantic novel *A Room with a View*, Forster projects the triumph of Love and Truth which is a recurrent theme of his work; the heroine of the novel marries a socially questionable young man, nullifying the conventions of the society. It also envisions man in a disjointed, inexplicable universe in search of wholeness and harmony; and the tininess and isolation of man in the universe; the contract between the two responses to life: one direct and vigorous, and the other vicarious and guarded, precisely, natural and artificial, comedy and prophecy, England/Sawston and Italy.

There is no cultural alternative to the pastoral setting of England; even Italy does not provide one. Here the passion and honesty of Forster is communicated through the character of Mr. Emerson, who can be called a Forsterian sage, warning Lucy against the muddle and helping save her from disaster like Mr. Failing of *The Longest Journey*; his humanism sharpened by the romantic sense of doom and conscious of the positive side of life, in search of order in chaos, and facing the everlasting Why and not a transitory *Yes*. The realism of Forster has both the positive and negative poles of an emotional charge. So *A Room with a View* begins with an expedition and culminates in the return.

Forster is essentially a novelist of middle class whether it is the case of English public school, the Cambridge University, Italy or Sawston; he talks of its values represented but the repressive and philistine section, its dogged industry, the English public school, its cultured and sensitive aspect represented by the Cambridge University, its class values, vitality, spontaneity and authenticity represented by Italy (Wlitshire), etc. He is aware of the growing materialism of the Edwardian Age and the challenge of the machine to traditional culture, precisely; both sociology and art which David Garnett calls Coleridgean urge to include everything. His idea of culture derives from the romantic tradition which finds culture both in society and individual as reaching perfection because it considers with nature and culture becomes man's equivalent for nature. He believes that in society and in individual the principle of polarity operates and this principle brings us close to tradition. At the same time, his moral thesis comprises the ideal of inconclusiveness and of connection of man with an allegorical contrast between the inner world of personal existence and the outer world of practical organization of living.

Obviously, Forster's writings divulge his codes, and his message can be extracted by decoding only, such as, the laws governing the conventional middle class, free from sectarian exclusiveness, the vitality of political life, his profound scepticism, the aptitude of individual goodness, a totally free individual. In his vision of ideal society. His voice is that of a humanist, of a liberal tradition, moral sericusness, of ethical values, of social censure, of individual imperative, of fusion of natural and social selves, of self-discovery and self-realization, of secular and spiritual salvation, of agnostic anxiety, of the validity of passion, of the romantic existential commitment, of eclecticism, of romantic yearning to include everything, of sceptical irony, of classical mythology, of visionary insight and of inconclusiveness at the end of the day—and here lies his article of faith.

References

Forster, E.M., 1936, *Abinger Harvest*, London: Edward Arnold.

______ ., 1951, *Two Cheers for Democracy*, London: Edward Arnold.

______ ., 1908, *A Room with a View*, London: Edward Arnold.

______ ., 1908, *The Hill of Devi*, London: Edward Arnold.

22

The Ride of Radicalism

Radicalism has been an obsession for progressives thinkers, philosophers and artists since long.[1] Contrary to the conviction that explains it as a negative force, this study seeks to prove it as a strong constructive force behind all momentous achievements of any culture and civilization. Primarily, it is the dormant urge of a man for change—in the political set-up, social structure, religious discipline, economic perceptions or artistic manifestations. It is the basic instinct of a man that rebels against the existing pattern and finally its triumph only brings a remarkable change or so-called development in that specific field, and the person advocating a particular cause turns a pioneer such, as Marx, Lenin, Gandhi, etc. It proves to be a continuous process for any growing individual, society or nation. To justify this proposition, the instance of the rise of USA as a supreme power of the world is cited here, as reflected in its history and literature, right from its emergence, dissecting the 1920s in particular. In history, it is implied in different turmoil's in the name of reformatory movements, whereas in literature it can be felt in the change of form, that is, style, technique, structure, treatment of theme, constitution of character and projection of voice.

The story of America starts with a dream, a vision—at times battered, redefined renewed, not of a foreordained national destiny unfolding effortlessly of a laborious struggle, rooted in hope. North America offered a haven for new beginnings. The new world of the West carried better prospect than the hard and tough life of the old redundant world of the East.

During the sixteenth and seventeenth century, the settlement of America took place as a by-product of the unsettlement of Europe. The turmoil of the Middle Ages, brought about by feudal lordships, was followed by Protestant Reformation and the Renaissance. It was the Renaissance spirit which inspired the Western Europe to move towards the West; to the undiscovered seas and lands, followed by other explorers. The records of Spanish Coronado, the French Father Hennepin and the British adventurer Captain John Smith tell the study of belittling hardships and overstating the possibilities of the future. They had impatient idealism to convert the Indians to Christianity and to capture their gold and land.

By the eighteenth century this new world had association of colonies, Protestant in religion, agricultural in economy and English in speech, with naive idealism and crude materialism. The seventeenth and eighteenth century America became the laboratory of ideas formed in English and Western Europe and implanted in America. The great religious, political and intellectual revolution that moved from the Renaissance and the Reformation into the Enlightenment and the Age of Reason became the pattern of everyday life. The fall and, restoration of the Stuart dynasty and the rise and fall of the Puritan Commonwealth determined in large part the characters of the first American colonies. The breakdown of the Middle Ages brought the idea of free individual whereas the Puritan orthodoxy floated the revolution theory of the rights of man.

The American Revolution was a crusade for human liberty, a private war between the Atlantic seaboard colonies and the present British nation. So started the fight for human rights and the concept of the sovereignty of the people, formulated by Locke, Hobbes, Shaftesbury, etc., became a threat to the British rule. 'The Declaration of Independence', the classic pronouncement on human rights was preceded by The Mayflower Compact (1620), The Hartford Constitution (1639), the First Continental Congress in Philadelphia (1774) and the Virginia Convention (1776) formed the basic American principle. The concept is contrary to the earlier belief of submission to external authority or belief in the sovereignty of God. America has constant concern for human liberty; there has always been a party of the extreme right and one of the extreme left. Jefferson, a great architect of American mind, wrote the intellectual foundations of the political and social system of a democracy founded upon independence. With Emerson and Thoreau came the faith in the individual as the measure of all religious liberalism, political democracy and literary romanticism: the political and literary. Scenario of the 20th century developed consistently with the progress of time.

The discovery of America, its emergence and grand march till date provides a history of 'fermentation' of the 'melting pot'—that was basically radical in nature. The Puritans and others who congregated, deserting their native land had a dream of better morrow. 'The Declaration of Independence' bears the spirit of urgent desire "that all men are created equal, that they are endowed by their creator with certain inalienable rights, that among these are life, liberty and pursuit of happiness." And it continued with the ideals as Alfred North Whitehead observed, "The health of people depends largely on their ability to question their inherited symbol in light of contemporary actualities, to keep them fluid, vibrant and responsive." Such optimistic note abounds in history, as in Jefferson's pronouncement, "The creator has made the earth for the living not for the dead", and Senator Platt's assertion.... "We live in a new creation... human society is full of creators."[3]

This all resulted in the belief that leads to creativity which ultimately brings advancement and change. "Central to the American vision of good society is the notion of individual freedom" and commitment to a social and intellectual process, of creating a just social order. As Josse doe la Cruz in 1980 felt, "We have to keep on struggling... hope dies last, You can't lose hope. If you lose hope, you lose everything." American psyche worked on continual movement, from sheer wanderlust and larking to speeding and driving into the distant and the unknown, that is, "a sign of energy and health." "Adventure, romance, thrill, challenge... authenticate man's love for change... a deep-seated desire for free, uncomplicated, unconventional life, American moksha or nirvana lied in action and engagement, not in static or stillness". "American dynamism and kinetic gets translated chiefly into picturesque novels and tales... brings to new focus the modern American's unlimited appetite for experience, change and movement... American love, of liberty and opportunity." At the higher levels of the society, it signified American search for refinement, tradition and heritage in the midst of increasing affluence. Out of the cultural clash of America and Europe, the nineteenth century. America was anxious for its cultural identity.

Americans view everything through the prism of their ideology that asserted revolution throught the globe: "It was the American flag that has brought about the peaceable revolution in Russia, it is the American flag that will bring about revolution in Germany.... It is the American ideal that dominate the world," concluded Des Moines Register on 23rd March 1917. Throughout the history we have conspicuous instances of the essential rebel sour of Americans that finally brought the enormous growth and progress of the country.

This study analyzes the 1920s as particular since American life manifesting the essence of Americanism because this specific decade stands for its brilliance in all spheres: literary experimentalism, cultural ebullience, social transformation, business ethics and radical creative exploration. The 1920s had experienced the failure of Woodrow Wilson's prophetic assurance to his countrymen that he was leading his peaceful people into war in order to foster the world-wide adoption of American democratic principles and forms: "for democracy, for the right of those who submit to the authority to have a voice in their own government, for the rights and liberties of small nations, for universal dominion of right."[6] As a result, they were disappointed and disillusioned. The post-war years not only made it difficult for ideas like cultural pluralism to take root, it led to the rejection of the 'melting pot' itself giving ample impetus to Americanization movement with its concept of national identity. In their immigration politics they exhibited a national urge, to turn backwards. Yet it was the dawn of a new era with its technology, automobiles, mass production and consumption, radio, movies and other forms of mass media, modern religious teaching in the churches, the enhanced political and cultural influence of large cities, new moral codes and standards—all taken together termed as 'acids of modernity' which were transforming the entire society. "Idealism and crusading zeal were still very much alive throughout the decade."[7]

Here idealism is used to define a movement that puts forward a set of principles about which people feel strongly enough to band together and fight for. The three movements were prohibitions, fundamentalism and the Klan which retained, reformist overtones, having the support of a large segment of the nation's progressives. President Coolidge's pronouncement that "The business of America is business... the man who builds a factory builds a temple" gave a new dimension to the economy. The political impulse was driven underground, and a dangerous ideal of free enterprise America ran unchecked. American lifestyle was totally changed with the dominance of Main Street, Prohibition, Red Scare and Ku Klux Klan. Obviously, it was a very radical age at the level of human consciousness and behaviour, termed as "behavioural experimentalism" as Fitzgerald admits; "Something subtle passed to America, the style of men."[8] "An entire survey of the American past serves only to reinforce the conviction that the Puritan, who had dominated history and was now fully in command of American life... the Puritan... pioneers... in one direction that of utilitarian ethics."[9]

Hung between the two severe political realities the First World War and the Great Depression, the decade is taken to be the most fertile period of American writing. A close examination of the literary works of the period gives the impression that they were disenchanted lot in search of something undefined, through transformation. This study is confined to the works of Hemingway and Fitzgerald. As explained earlier, radicalism in literature is understood on two levels: first its experimental nature and the second in its distinct voice of contemporary involvement with the times, that is, social criticism.

The experimental aim is to capture new consciousness, new pace and new relationship. In Fitzgerald's *Tender is the Night*, Dick Diver immerses himself in the urbanized centralized society of his time and tries to redeem it by living through it. In Hemingway's *The Sun also Rises*, Jack Barnes shares the universe of the modern community and tries to make an economic and personal destiny within it. They conceived the American past as a timeless ideal. The experimentation becomes so prevalent a style in American writing that it is virtually the style of changing

America. Fitzgerald bound himself tightly to the glossy and wealthy cosmopolitan fife which was a species of the decades experimentalism. His first novel, *This Side of Paradise*, is taken to be the stance of style-setter for the times. His power to stand back and criticise is out of his own painful experience and effort. His stories bear a "touch of disaster". Nick Caraway, the narrator in *The Great Gatsby*, stills the voice of judgment, explores the complexities of a there and finds Gatsby morally unsatisfactory at all levels. Gatsby is derivative of this world who is gradually distinguished from it and set against it, so that finally he becomes victim of contingency. Fitzgerald's effects are surreal coming out of the drean-world after its withdrawal.

The new post-war generation came to terms with the naturalistic tradition represented by Dresser and Anderson, guided by the belief that it was the writer's responsibility to expose and hopefully to correct the shortcomings and injustices of contemporary American society by providing an account of social criticism. Dresser carried the spirit of Marxism and Anderson the new psychology of individual behaviour guided by Freud—it all provided a new way of observing the relationship between the individual and the society. They shared a common belief that the novelist must be not only a responsible artist but also a responsible critic of society. "They turned to the unfashionable form of tragedy as a means of dramatizing the eternal conflict between the individual and society, and attained in their fiction a more complex and more satisfying form for social criticism and a far greater artistic distinction than that to be found in the naturalistic tradition."[3] The implication of Henry James comment, that to be an American is a tragic destiny, is explored in the fiction of the 1920s as intellectual achievement. Gatsby's dream is shattered in the shabby moral limitations of the society. Dick Diver of *Tender is the Wight* embodies all aspirations of the cultivated, dominant 'American Establishment' committed to the creative social leadership of a colony of rich expatriate Americans who fell victim to his inherent limitations of commitment, and disintegrates as a personality and a tragic hero. Fitzgerald attempts to be with an important aspect of American society as a tragic experience. The development of Hemingway's novels from naturalism to the tragic vision is most conspicuous in *The Sun also Rises* and *A Farewell to Arms*. The characters are innocent victims of the shabby war and stupid peace, and finally withdraw themselves as individuals and man is ultimately left alone.

In *To Have and Have Not*, Harry reaches the conclusion that survival by oneself is no longer possible. In *For Whom the Boll Tolls*, Jordans' heroic nature is of tragic commitment. *The Old Man and the Sea* reveals the limitation of tragedy—not as a means of life but as a means of life but as a means of imaginative writer to make certain fundamental aspects of life meaningful. There is a conflict between one's responsibilities to the society and to one's own self. Robert Jodan's struggle to make a better world by fighting for a cause fails and brings about destruction. Fitzgerald's puritanical soul rebelled when his love affair with Ginevra King ended in crushing disappointment and he noted in his *Ledger* (1916), "Poor boys shouldn't think of marrying rich girls" and he denounces the age. As he acquires wealth, he adopts romantic radicalism. The entire globe polarizing around wealth and poverty, purity and corruption, youth and age is reflected in *This Side of Paradise*, Fitzgerald is the most uncomfortable man of his times.

The writers of the 1920 are radical in their spirit and work, and three quests, "the quest of survival, identity and authenticity", an intellectual movement apparent in their writing. Richard Chase admits that American novel was born out of "aesthetic possibilities of radical forms"[9] and Malcolm Bradbury accepted "We were radicals in literature".

Notes and References

1. Radicalism has been defined variously, as "a political stance advocating fundamental change in the existing political, economic and social order... challenge to established privilege" (*Academic American Encyclopedia*, Vol. 16, pp. 43-44); "a doctrine that advocates going to the root of a problem... advocates extreme solutions." (*Joy of Knowledge*, Vol. II, K-Z, p. 597); "intellectual innovation used for action" (*The American Novel*, M. Bradbury (3d.) Aronold Heiman, 1980, p. 11).
2. Park H.B., 1964, *United States of America: A History,* Scientific Book Agencies. p. 745.
3. Bradbury M. (ed.), 1980, *American Novel,* Arnold Helman.
4. Boyer, P.S., 1990, *Enduring Vision,* Vol. II, D.C. Health & Co.
5. Maini, D.S., 1988, *Spirit of American Literature.* Sterling Pub., p. 8.
6. Lawrence, L.W., *Defender of the Faith.* New York, Ch. 5-9.
7. Fitzgerald, F.S., *Jass Age in the Crack-Up.*
8. Hoffman, F.J., 1955, *Twenties,* Viking, pp. 29-31.
9. Bhalla, B.M. (ed.), 1981, *Twentieth Century America Novel,* Kalyani Pub. p.7.

23

Naipaul's Self in His Half a Life

Naipaul's work may justifiably be read as an autobiography of his diaspora self, and the construction of diasporic imagery or self requires the mnemonic mediation that may connect the past with the present and also address the future. Both his fiction and non-fiction reveal his diaspora consciousness to recollect and re-construct plenty of metaphors to explain the harrowing realities of a multicultural and multilingual civilization *Half a Life* is his recent novel that inscribes a fragmented self, situated in the troubled history of ethnic hatred and discrimination, exile and dispossession, homelessness and frustration. The present paper seeks to define his tenets that constitute his writing, particularly the recent outburst, *Half a Life*.

In his reception speech to the Nobel Committee and the Swedish Academy in Stockholm on 7, December 2001, Naipaul admits:

> Everything of value about me is in my books... I will say I am the sum of my books. Each book, intuitively sensed and, in the ease of fiction, intuitively worked out, stands on what has gone before, and grows out of it at any stage of my literary career. It could have been said, that the last book contained all others... both fiction and the travel book form has given me my way of looking....

Naipaul explains his motive, as pointed out by Tejpal:

> My kind of writing tries to find a spring, the motion of societies and cultures... so it's that refinement of emotions that really makes the writing, what you call understanding. (Tejpal, Web page)

Half a Life has three sections, representing three stages of life, as past, present and future, and almost synonymous to the progression of his own life and yet incomplete; in fact, it is simply a step forward with a few sketches, and his previous works comprising the earlier drawings it is all about "half made societies and half made nations". The birth of a protagonist out of a Brahmin and a low caste woman, his uncommon naming that has alien borrowing and his shifting to other countries bears a typical post-colonial impression of hybridity, temporality and displacement; he is a victim and not a welcome in his own family, by his own parents:

> We've created a monster. He really hates his mother and his mother's people, and she doesn't know. But his mother's uncle was firebrand of the backwards, I mustn't forge that. The boy will poison what remains of my life. I must get him far away from here. (41-42)

Virtually he has been kicked out of the family in the name of studies abroad; as an old-fashioned Indian allows the growth of his son as per his choices and attitudes, to shape his perception and personality, to face the trials of the world both ulterior and exterior, to launch in the unacquainted world; his nourishment is not a usual one. The first section of the book entitled 'A Visit from Somerset Maugham' is also interpreted as a satirical rewriting of R. K. Narayan's *The Guide*, for instance, the father of Willie escaping the persecution of the local king and taking refuge in a temple courtyard "living as a mendicant on the alms of the poorest of the poor" (3), visit of Somerset Maugham in the temple courtyard, etc. His departure to England, is a search for identity/

self/solace in the name of higher education and like Naipaul wanders the streets of London as inexperienced and immigrant to settle at freelancing job with the BBC. Willie's outburst of creativity, his making as a writer also resembles that of Naipaul; in a few stories that he wrote initially, with his memory of his childhood in rural India, we find something peculiar,

> The stories seemed to be just waiting for him; he was surprised he hadn't seen them before; and he wrote fast for three or four weeks. The writing then began to lead him to difficult things, things he couldn't face, and he stopped. (96)

Ana, Naipaul's wife, is attracted by the stories before the her marriage, because she finds something synonymous to her own life:

> That was just before I met you. I think you will see now why your stories spoke to me. All the bluff, the make believe, with the real unhappiness. It was unnecessary; it was why I wrote. (146)

Things keep on growing, multiplying, call it development or anything else. Willie's past remains a mystery and as he grows he tries to forget whatever he knows, prefers to live in a world of hallucination; it is simply to construct something that he pretends; it is Naipaul's search of self: "The story changed as Willie grew up. Things were added and by the time Willie left India to go to England this was the story he had heard." (1)

Even in his Nobel Lecture, Naipual talks of his childhood experiences of cultural loss that finally takes the form of cultural confusion pointing out his ignorance and indifference of his Trinidadian family. The influence of his father is immense. As Willie finds in the first section of *Half a Life* and Naipaul in one of his interviews.

> The writing that has mattered most to me is that of my father, which has been published. It taught me to look at things which was been written about before; and seemed dull in life, yet when transferred to paper became very surprising. (Salgado, 1987, 317)

Willie's life is synonymous with the biographical note, which Naipaul contributed to his works published by Penguin: V.S. Naipaul was born in Trinidad in 1932. He came to England in 1950 to do a university course and began to write in London, in 1954. He has followed no other profession.

The second section of the book is significant as it provides something exclusive to Willie's life in London, a writer in making, a platform for the growth of creativity similar to that of Naipaul. It was entirely a new world, unacquainted, illusionary, unprohibited, preventive, provoking, mysterious and yet full of possibilities.

> ...he was free to present himself as he wished. He could, as it were, write his own revolution. The possibilities were dizzying. He could within reason, remake himself and his past and his ancestry. (62)

Shortly after his arrival in London, Willie discovers that he has "to relearn everything that he knew". He starts playing with words. Though the passion of writing was discovered much before coming to England, the literary bohemia of the late fifties of England furnished an opportunity to invent stories about his background; it was a sort of borrowed identity. Willie admits the inspiration of Hemingway's short stories, *The Killers*, both the text and the film, in his first attempt of story writing and he feels that it is easier to thrive in the field of writing with borrowed settings, themes, and characters than to focus a slice of his own life. The first victim/admirer is Ana, the future wife who has been trapped, unable to recognize the artificiality of plot and hypocrisy of presentation and Willie can diagnose very easily:

> ...if she came and questioned him too closely about his book, he might find himself giving the game away, and the woman or girl might under stand that the Indian stories in which she had seen aspects of her own African life had been borrowed from old Hollywood movie and the Maxim hanky triology from Russia. Willie did not want the woman to be let down he wanted her to stay an admirer. (125)

In her letter to Willie, Ana explains the similarity that she in between his stories and her own life:

> I feel, I had to write to you because in your stories for the first time I find moments that are like moments in my life, though the background and material are so different, It does my heart a lot of good to think that out there all these years there was someone thinking and feeling like me. (124)

Naipaul emphasizes his passion of remaking elsewhere too, "...we remade the world for our self; every generation does that, as we found when we come together." (Naipaul, 1987, 318) This tendency persists in Naipaul, "My theme, the narrative to carry it, my characters—for some years I felt, they were sitting on my shoulder, waiting to declare themselves and to possess me." (1987: 309)

In fact, on the very first page of *Half a Life* he clarifies the intention: "This book is an invention. It is not exact about the countries, periods or situations it appears to describe." Contrary to his confusion he projects his own self throughout the novel, right from the mysterious background, developing in his artistic frame and writing skill and life afterwards.

The three sections of *Half a Life* represent the three aspects of Naipaul's own life, his childhood, his education and the formative forces that made him a writer; we may call it striking autobiographical element, or search of self, or a voice of Diaspora or post-colonial revolutionary or radical self-description; in fact, he translates his own experience in his work.

Obviously *Half a Life* comprises sorrow of exile, projection of family history and a typical post-colonial anguish, in different shades and evaluation, applicable to Naipaul himself, manifested in the character of Willie Chandran. Violation of social and moral ethics by his father haunts Willie throughout his life; consequently, he fails at life as well as love, and appears as character of failed fulfilment, a pessimist. Naipaul is Willie as well as his counterpart, devoid of self-determination, spirituality, the power of resistance, social and moral ethics, and all that counts for his inner development. On contrary, he compromises with the traits of individuality, intellectuality, free choice, self-responsibility, physical gratification, deceit, pride, hypocrisy, and egocentric, though he fails to embrace an all-encompassing theme, betraying self-denial and search for meaning. The agility of his observation forms his personal ethics, trans-cultural and critical. Even Gandhi is not spared and his influence on Willie's father is disastrous; he is a victim of ideology and hence there is no substantial reason behind his marriage to a low caste woman or professional misconduct, destroying files at his office or finding refuge in a temple and taking a vow of silence. Though he is a cunning bluffer, he remains composed in his silence. Willie's need of reconstruction of identity is out of the idea of social and cultural differences, hovering between acceptance and rejection "as a man and being in his own eyes compete" but the introduction of Graca and June, and the subsequent sexual gratification seems to be out of place, though it reveals the possibility of a shifting life and multiculturalism. As explained by Bruce King, Naipaul,

> ...feels humiliated by the weakness and exploitation of the colonized; the blames European imperialism for the problems it left for colonies, while praising it for bring peace and modern thought of the world that remained medieval and debilitated by continual There is a moral honesty in his work, a refusal to sentimentalize England on the former colonies. (2)

Willie is allowed to suffer and realize the fate of a displaced like Naipaul, his failures and futile endeavours: "I have been hiding from myself. I have been hiding from myself. I have risked nothing. And now the best part of my life is over." (130)

Significantly, Naipaul defends his protagonist Willie, his identity and integrity, amidst all the turbulence of cultural collisions, moral fragmentation, individual anxieties, rational intellectuality and compulsive homelessness, as Willie tells Ana:

> When I asked you in London I was frightened. I had nowhere to go. They were going to throw me out of the college at the end of the term and I didn't now what I could do to keep afloat...But now the best part of my life has gone, and I've done nothing." (127-28)

Willie is unanchored like Naipaul and voices the sense of loss, inauthenticity, uncertainty, confusion and a sense of rejection, and at the same time it is also an assertion of one's dignity. He is "reborn" in England as a writer based on the perception of the circumstances; in *A Way in the World*, he points out, "...to the very beginning; in our blood and bone and brain we carry the memories of thousands of beings... we cannot understand all the traits we have inherited. Sometimes we can be strangers to ourselves." (11)

Naipaul is essentially a writer of diaspora and the plot of *Half a Life*, that is, plight of immigrants of imperial colonies and displacement of migratory people recur in most of his works, as Pranjape points out:

> Since diaspora writing emanates from identity formation leading to further and more sophisticated articulations of identity, or manifest in community, nationhood, and also larger global contexts, it is important to remember perceive diaspora space as at all time explanatory, fluid and dynamic so that intersections within histories, past and futures, do not congeal into rigid boundary laden states." (Pranjape, 2001. 159)

Naipaul is an expatriate individual, uprooted, fragmented and twisted and his state of permanent exile finds place in his work as manifestation of 'self'; and as Homi Bhabha tells us, "hyhridization, migration and globalization". *Half a Life* stands very close to Naipaul and Willie resembles Naipaul in many respects.

References

King, Bruce., 1993, *V.S. Naipaul*, London: Macmillan.

Naipaul, V.S., 2001, "Two Worlds", Nobel Lecture, 7 Dec.

______ ., 1995, *A Way in the World*, New York: Vintage.

______ ., 2001, *Half a Life*, Knopf.

______ ., 1987, *The Enigma alArrival*, Hammondsport: Penguin.

Pranjape. M., (ed.), 2001, *I am Diaspora, Theories, Histories, Texts*, New Delhi: Indian Pub.

Salgado, G., 1987, "V.S. Naipaul and the Politics of Fiction," *The New Peliean Guide to English Literature.* (ed.), Boris Ford, Penguin Books.

Tejpal T.J., "V. S. Naipaul's *A Way in the World*", Random House, Web Page.

Index